350
MOST COMMON
SAT
VOCABULARY

Copyright © 2025 Author BrainWorks Society
First published in 2025 by SharonShine Books

SharonShine Books
14-12, Teheran-ro 78-gil,
Gangnam-gu, Seoul 06194
Republic of Korea
www.sharonshine.com
Instagram: @brainworks_society_official

ISBN: 979-11-984601-7-2

Advisors
Sharon Kang, Melissa Kim

Student Lead Author
Annabelle Cho (Grade 11, Fayston Preparatory of Suji, Korea)

Student Co-Authors
Mia Song (Grade 11, Prestige School Toronto Campus, Canada)
Jason Song (Grade 11, Prestige School Toronto Campus, Canada)
Ray Han (Grade 11, Glenbrook North High School, IL)
Lauren Yoon (Grade 10, Glenbrook North High School, IL)
Ethan Kim (Grade 10, Glenbrook North High School, IL)

Student Designers/Editors
Seojin Oh (Grade 9, Eastern Technical High School, MD)
Christine Lee (Grade 9, Hanover High School, NH)
Annie Woo and Yedam Kim (Grade 11, Fayston Preparatory of Suji, Korea)

Created by high school students who achieved over 1500

350 MOST COMMON

SAT

VOCABULARY

Designed to Maximize

Memory Retention

STUDENT-APPROVED

- ☑ *Personal Checklist*
- ☑ *Review Quiz*
- ☑ *Definitions + Synonyms*
- ☑ *Example Sentences*

SETTING

Personal Checklist

DAILY GOAL
How many words will I learn each study day?
[ ] 10 [ ] 15 [ ] 20 [ ] 25 [ ] Other: _____

WEEKLY GOAL
Target words this week: [ ] 50 [ ] 70 [ ] 100 [ ] Other: _____
Study days: [ ] Mon [ ] Tue [ ] Wed [ ] Thu [ ] Fri [ ] Sat [ ] Sun
Preferred time: [ ] Morning [ ] Afternoon [ ] Evening
Time window: _____-_____

CHOOSE A METHOD (choose the ones you'll use)
[ ] Handwrite Headlist (Gold List)
[ ] Distill after ~14 days (D1)
[ ] Mini-sentences (3 per day)
[ ] Roots/affixes note (1-2 per word)
[ ] 60-sec recall aloud (light)
[ ] Quick quiz (Fri/Sat)
[ ] Flashcards/app (max ____ min/day)

GOLD LIST DATES (write your actual dates)
Start date (Headlist): _____
Distill 1: Start date + 14 days → _____
Distill 2: Distill 1 + 14 days → _____
Distill 3: Distill 2 + 14 days → _____

MASTERY = I can··· (define what "mastered" means for me)
[ ] give a correct definition
[ ] use it in a sentence
[ ] give 1 synonym or antonym
[ ] spell it correctly
Other: _____

QUIZ & TARGETS
Weekly quiz score goal: ____ / ____   Retake if < ____%
Words I expect to master this week: _____ / _____

REWARD
Weekly reward when I hit my goal:
_____

NAME:

Signature: _____   Date: _____

4

7- WEEK SAT VOCAB PLAN

WEEK 1
1-50

WEEK 2
51 - 100

WEEK 3
101 - 150

WEEK 4
151 - 200

WEEK 5
201 - 250

WEEK 6
251 - 300

WEEK 7
301 - 350

How to Maximize your Memory Retention

Follow these steps for fast and maximum results

Write a little every day
Learn 10-20 new words per study day. Handwrite them with definitions, examples, or root notes. Writing itself strengthens memory.

Review every 14 days
Leave your list untouched for 14 days, then rewrite only the hard words. Repeat this distillation 3 times to lock words into long-term memory.

Test yourself actively
Say meanings aloud, make short example sentences, and quiz yourself on Fridays/Saturdays. Use flashcards/apps in short, focused bursts.

Set weekly goals
Aim for 50-100 words per week (70 is ideal). Take a quiz and retake if below your target. True mastery means you can define, spell, use in a sentence, and give a synonym/antonym.

Reward your progress
Give yourself a small weekly reward when you hit your goal. Consistency is your greatest weapon.

Summary Box Write your own summary

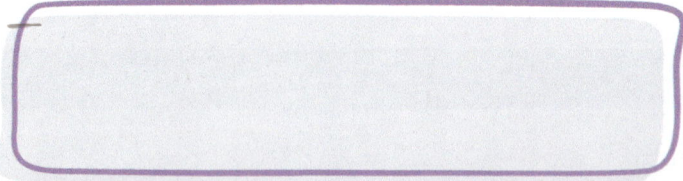

6

Abate

To lessen in intensity or degree.

Synonyms: Lessen, reduce

1. Instead of waiting at home for the pain to abate, we decided to go to the emergency room, even though it was midnight.

2. Hoping to abate his anger, she quickly apologized for the mistake

Verb

Abberation

A deviation from what is normal or expected.

Synonyms: Abnormality, oddity

1. The sudden drop in temperatures was an aberration from the usual mild weather in the region.

2. Her kind behavior was an aberration in a world that often seemed harsh and unforgiving.

Noun

Abhor

To regard with horror or loathing; to hate.

Synonyms: Detest, despise

3

Verb

1. As a vegetarian, she abhors the thought of eating meat.

2. He abhors dishonesty and always values truthfulness in his friendships.

Abridge

To shorten a piece of writing without losing its essence.

Synonyms: Shorten, curtail

4

Verb

1. She had to abridge several sections of her paper while preserving the main arguments.

2. The professor asked the students to abridge their essays to fit within the 1,000-word limit.

Abscond

To leave hurriedly and secretly.

Synonyms: Flee, escape

Verb

1. After taking the money, the thief absconded into the night.

2. After breaking the window he would abscond to avoid being caught.

Abstruse

Difficult to understand.

Synonyms: Profound, cryptic

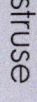

Adj.

1. The professor's lecture on quantum mechanics was so abstruse that only a few students could grasp its meaning.

2. Despite hours of studying, Jake still found the mathematical proof too abstruse to comprehend.

Accentuate

Accentuate

To emphasize or highlight.

Synonyms: Emphasize, underline

7

Verb

1. The designer used bold colors to accentuate the beauty of the dress.

2. The speaker's powerful tone and expressive gestures accentuated the importance of his message.

Acquiesce

Acquiesce

To agree reluctantly but without a protest.

Synonyms: Consent, comply

8

Verb

1. Although their initial plan was to demand compensation, they had to acquiesce due to the powerful authority of the opposing company.

2. After a long discussion, he finally acquiesced to his friend's request to join the trip to Italy.

Acrimonious

Full of anger, arguments, and bad feeling.

Synonyms: Bitter, caustic

1. The debate became increasingly acrimonious as both sides refused to compromise.

2. Their acrimonious divorce left them unable to speak to each other for years.

Adroit

Skillful, expert in the use of hands or mind.

Synonyms: Handy, dexterous

1. The scientist was adroit at handling delicate lab equipment.

2. She was adroit at drawing, making beautiful pictures with ease.

Adversity

A state of hardship or misfortune.

Synonyms: Misfortune, difficulty

11

Noun

1. Despite facing great adversity, she managed to complete her degree with honors.

2. The team showed incredible resilience in overcoming adversity to win the championship.

Alleviate

To relieve or lessen.

Synonyms: Reduce, ease

12

Verb

1. His sickness is going to eventually alleviate after getting the right treatment.

2. His anxiety was alleviated after he found out his dog was alive.

Altruistic

Unselfishly concerned for the welfare of others.

Synonyms: Selfless, generous

Adj.

1. Emma's altruistic nature led her to volunteer at the shelter every weekend, always putting others before herself.

2. The billionaire's altruistic donation helped fund schools and hospitals in underprivileged communities.

Ambiguous

Open to more than one interpretation.

Synonyms: Obscure, vague

Adj.

1. Her response was ambiguous, leaving everyone unsure whether she agreed or disagreed with the proposal.

2. The painting's ambiguous message sparked different kinds of interpretations.

Ambivalent

Having mixed or opposing feelings or attitudes towards something.

Synonyms: Conflicted, uncertain

15

Adj.

1. He was ambivalent about whether he was genuinely happy for the success of his coworker.

2. Experts have conducted numerous analyses of social media due to its ambivalent effects on both society and individuals.

Ameliorate

To improve or make something (unsatisfactory) better.

Synonyms: Mitigate, enhance

16

Verb

1. The government introduced new policies to ameliorate the economic crisis.

2. She tried to ameliorate the tense situation with a well-timed joke.

Amicable

Friendly and without conflict.

Synonyms: Friendly, cordial

17

Adj.

1. Even after their disagreement, they maintained an amicable relationship.

2. The neighbors had an amicable chat while gardening together.

Anachronistic

Out of place in time; not in chronological order.

Synonyms: Outmoded, archaic

18

Adj.

1. The use of a typewriter in a modern office felt anachronistic, as everyone else was using computers.

2. His outfit, which included a powdered wig and tricorn hat, seemed anachronistic in the 21st century.

Antithesis

The direct opposite of something.

Synonyms: Opposite, contrast

19

Noun

⭐

1. Her kindness was the antithesis of his cruelty.

2. The first performance was the antithesis of the last game.

Apathy

Lack of emotion, interest, and motivation.

Synonyms: Indifference, disinterest

20

Noun

⭐

1. The student's apathy toward his studies was evident in his lack of participation and missing assignments.

2. Despite the urgent crisis, the mayor's apathy frustrated citizens who expected swift action.

Apt

Suitable, likely, or quick to learn.

Synonyms: Suitable, relevant

21

Adj.

1. Her apt reply to the tricky question impressed everyone.

2. Given his experience, he was the apt choice for the leadership position.

Alarcity

Brisk and cheerful readiness; promptness in response.

Synonyms: Emagerness, enthusiasm

22

Noun

1. She accepted the invitation at the conference with surprising alacrity.

2. Despite the early hour, the team began the project with alarcity, excited to tackle the challenge.

Arduous

Involving or requiring strenuous effort; difficult.

Synonyms: Difficult, strenuous

1. Climbing the steep mountain was an arduous journey that tested their endurance.

2. Studying for the SAT while juggling extracurricular activities can be an arduous task.

23

Adj.

⭐

Ascertain

To find out or learn with certainty.

Synonyms: Determine, discover

1. He wanted to ascertain the truth before making any decisions.

2. After reviewing the data, she could ascertain that the hypothesis was correct.

24

Verb

Aspire

To direct one's hopes or ambitions toward achieving.

Synonyms: Desire, hope

1. She aspires to become a doctor and help underserved communities around the world.

2. Many young athletes aspire to compete in the Olympics one day, dedicating years to training.

Assiduous

Showing great care and perseverance.

Synonyms: Diligent, careful

1. She was assiduous in her studies, always working hard to achieve her goals.

2. His assiduous effort to improve his skills paid off when he won the competition.

Astute

Clever or shrewd.

Synonyms: Insightful, perceptive

27

Adj.

1. The astute investor quickly recognized the potential of the startup and made a profitable early investment.

2. Her astute observations during the debate allowed her to counter every argument effectively.

Audacious

Bold, daring, or fearless.

Synonyms: Fearless, defiant

28

Adj.

1. His audacious decision to start a new business during a recession shocked many, but it paid off in the end.

2. The audacious plan to climb the mountain without guides drew both admiration and concern from his peers.

Avarice

Extreme greed for wealth or material gain

Synonyms: Greed, materialism

29

Noun

1. I recently read a book where the main character ends up in the most miserable situation because of his avarice.

2. Many people expected the collapse of the empire, as the king's avarice was boundless.

Aversion

A strong dislike or disinclination.

Synonyms: Dislike, repulsion

30

Noun

1. She has a strong aversion to loud noises and always avoids crowded places.

2. Despite his aversion to public speaking, he delivered a compelling presentation.

Banal

So lacking in originality as to be obvious and boring.

Synonyms: Profound, cryptic

31

Adj.

1. The movie was so banal that she guessed the ending within the first ten minutes.

2. His speech was filled with banal phrases that everyone had heard before.

Belie

To fail to give a true impression of something.

Synonyms: Contradict, disprove

32

Verb

1. His calm demeanor belies the intense pressure he's under at work.

2. The warmth of the sun outside belies the chilly wind blowing through the streets.

Belligerent

Hostile or combative.

Synonyms: Aggressive, pugnacious

Adj.

1. His belligerent attitude made it difficult to have a calm conversation.

2. His belligerent tone during the meeting made everyone uncomfortable.

Benevolent

Well-meaning and kindly.

Synonyms: Charitable, compassionate

Adj.

1. The benevolent teacher stayed after school to help students who were struggling with their assignments.

2. The benevolent acts, like donating to charities and volunteering, made him well-loved in the community.

Benign

Gentle, kind; (of a disease) not harmful.

Synonyms: Kindly, warmhearted

35

Verb

1. Despite his intimidating appearance, the old man has a benign personality.

2. The tumor that she had was benign and posed no serious risk.

Bequeath

To hand down or leave in a will.

Synonyms: Bestow, leave (to)

36

Adj.

1. My friend is looking for a specialized lawyer to prevent his brother from attempting to bequeath all the assets to himself.

2. The painter bequeathed some of his masterpieces to the national museum so that they could be preserved for future generations.

Blatant

Done openly and unashamedly; obvious.

Synonyms: Charitable, compassionate

37

Adj.

1. He made a blatant mistake during the presentation.

2. It was a blatant lie, and everyone knew it.

Blithe

Showing a casual, cheerful indifference considered improper; happy and joyous.

Synonyms: Lighthearted, indifferent

38

Adj.

1. She was blithe about the risks of her health.

2. She gave a blithe response to the serious question, which made the others question her sincerity.

Bolster

To support or strengthen.

Synonyms: Support, boost

39

Verb

⭐

1. The company's new marketing campaign is designed to bolster its brand image.

2. Her kind words helped bolster his confidence before the big presentation.

Brevity

The quality of being brief or concise.

Synonyms: Conciseness, succinctness

40

Noun

⭐

1. The speaker was praised for the brevity of his presentation, getting straight to the point.

2. The brevity of her speech made a strong impact on the audience.

Bucolic

Relating to the countryside; rustic.

Synonyms: Pastoral, rural

Adj.

1. The bucolic landscape, with its rolling hills and peaceful streams, was the perfect setting for a relaxing weekend getaway.

2. She longed for a bucolic life on a farm, away from the hustle and bustle of the city.

Burgeon

To grow or develop quickly.

Synonyms: Expand, flourish

42

Verb

1. Her interest in science began to burgeon after she got her first lab kit.

2. The small startup quickly burgeoned into a huge company.

Buttress

A source of support or reinforcement.

Synonyms: Support, reinforce

1. The clear evidence suggested by the attorney helped to buttress the claim of innocence.

2. Due to the revised law, the building needs to have more buttresses per level.

Cajole

To persuade through flattery or promises.

Synonyms: Persuade, coax

1. She managed to cajole her friend into joining the dance competition despite his reluctance.

2. The salesman tried to cajole the customer into buying the more expensive model.

Candor

The quality of being open and honest.

Synonyms: Frankness, openness

1. The teacher appreciated the student's candor when asking for help on the difficult assignment.

2. The politician earned respect for his candor when addressing the issues facing the country.

Capricious

Impulsive or unpredictable.

Synonyms: Inconsistent, unstable

1. His capricious nature made it difficult for the team to rely on his decisions.

2. The weather in the mountains can be capricious, changing from sunny to stormy in an instant.

Catalyst

Something that causes change.

Synonyms: Spart, trigger

Noun

1. Her suggestion was the catalyst for the team's new approach to the project.

2. His idea acted as a catalyst for the team to start working more efficiently

Censure

Strong disapproval or criticism.

Synonyms: Reprimand, condemnation

Noun

1. The senator faced censure from her colleagues after her controversial comments during the debate.

2. The company issued a formal censure against the employee for violating the code of conduct.

Chicanery

The use of trickery to achieve a political, financial, or legal purpose.

Synonyms: Deception, trickery

1. The politician's chicanery misled voters into supporting them.

2. The salesman used chicanery to sell overpriced products.

Chronic

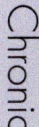

(Of an illness or a problem) persisting for a long time or constantly recurring.

Synonyms: Long-term, continual

1. She suffers from a chronic disease that she was diagnosed with when she was three years old.

2. During the pandemic, a chronic shortage of medical supplies was a big problem.

350
SAT
VOCAB

1-50
REVIEW

Multiple Choice Synonyms

1. What is a synonym of *alleviate?*

a) worsen
b) relieve
c) ignore
d) initiate

2. What is a synonym of *audacious?*

a) cautious
b) timid
c) bold
d) lazy

3. What is a synonym of *banal?*

a) original
b) dull
c) exciting
d) obscure

4. What is a synonym of *benevolent?*

a) selfish
b) kind
c) harsh
d) beneficial

Fill-in-the-Blank

5. Although the two countries had their differences, they maintained an _ _ _ _ _ _ relationship through diplomacy.

a) amicable   b) arduous   c) belligerent   d) ascertain

6. The professor's explanation of quantum theory was so _ _ _ _ _ _ that even advanced students struggled to understand it.

a) adroit   b)abtruse   c) apt   d) capricious

7. The lobbyist's use of legal _ _ _ _ _ _ _ _ delayed the vote for months.

a) blatant   b) catalyst   c) Chicanery   d) Buttress

1-50 Review

True or False

8. The boy's avarice for knowledge made him read five books a week

T   F

9. Her astute observations during the debate impressed the judges.

T   F

10. The invention of the smartphone was a *catalyst* for major changes in the way people communicate and access information.

T   F

Matching the words and definitions

Abhor   To improve or make something better

Brevity   The quality of being brief or precise

Chicanery   To regard with horror or loathing

Ameliorate   The use of trickery to achieve political, financial, or legal purpose.

Write Synonyms   Write down synonyms for the following words

Abscond

_____

Acrimonious

_____

Assiduous

_____

Blatant

_____

Censure

_____

Crossword Puzzle

DOWN

1. To accept or agree to something passively.

3. The direct opposite or a strong contrast between two things.

4. A deviation from the normal or expected; something unusual or out of the ordinary.

5. Honesty or openness, especially in expressing opinions or feelings.

6. To support, strengthen, or reinforce.

8. Kind, gentle, or harmless (often used medically to mean not dangerous).

ACROSS

2. To reduce in intensity or amount.

7. To emphasize or make more noticeable.

9. Hostile and aggressive; ready to fight.

10. To give a false impression of something; to contradict.

Clairvoyant

Able to perceive things beyond normal senses.

Synonyms: Psychic, prophetic

51

Noun
Adj.

1. The clairvoyant claimed she could see the future, but skeptics dismissed her predictions.

2. His clairvoyant instincts helped him make the right investment decisions at the right time.

Clemency

Mercy or leniency.

Synonyms: Mildness, indulgence

52

Noun

1. The president granted clemency to the prisoners, giving them a second chance at life.

2. She hoped for clemency from her teacher after missing the deadline due to illness.

Coalesce

To come together and form one mass or whole.

Synonyms: Unite, combine

1. Over time, the different factions within the company began to coalesce around a single vision for the future.

2. The diverse musical influences in the band's latest album coalesce into a unique sound that appeals to a wide audience.

Coerce

To force or intimidate.

Synonyms: Pressure, constrain

1. The boss tried to coerce his employees into working overtime.

2. They tried to coerce him into signing the contract, but he refused.

Cogent

Clear, logical, and convincing.

Synonyms: Rational, objective

55

Adj.

1. The lawyer presented a cogent argument that convinced the jury of her client's innocence.

2. His cogent explanation of the complex topic made it easy for everyone to understand.

Colloquial

Characteristic of informal speech or writing.

Synonyms: Conversational, casual

56

Adj.

1. His speech was full of colloquial expressions that made it feel casual and relatable

2. The book's colloquial language made it easier for readers to read it.

Concur

To agree or have the same opinion.

Synonyms: Accord, coincide

1. Although we have been best friends for many years, we do not always concur with each other when it comes to academic plans.

2. Despite the recurring conferences, the representatives of the nations could not concur on the issue.

Condone

To accept or allow behavior that is morally wrong.

Synonyms: Disregard, accept

1. The teacher refused to **condone** cheating and immediately reported the students involved.

2. By staying silent, he seemed to **condone** the unethical behavior of his colleagues.

Confound

To confuse or perplex.

Synonyms: Astonish, amaze

59

Verb

⭐

1. The unexpected results of the experiment **confounded** the scientists.

2. His strange behavior continued to **confound** his friends, who couldn't figure out what was going on.

◆

Conscientious

Diligent and careful.

Synonyms: Sedulous, dedicated

Adj.

1. She's a conscientious student who always double-checks her work to ensure it's accurate.

2. The conscientious doctor took the time to explain the treatment plan in detail, making sure the patient understood every step.

Contempt

Disrespect or disdain.

Synonyms: Scorn, neglect

1. She looked at the rude comment with utter contempt.

2. She looked at the unfair decision with clear contempt.

61

Noun

⭐

Convoluted

Extremely complex and difficult to follow.

Synonyms: Inconsistent, unstable

1. The instructions for assembling the furniture were so convoluted that I had to ask for help.

2. The professor's convoluted lecture left the students confused and unsure of the main points.

62

Adj.

Copious

Abundant or plentiful.

Synonyms: Ample, profuse

1. She took copious notes during the lecture to ensure she didn't miss anything

2. The garden produced a copious amount of vegetables this season.

Corroborate

To confirm or give support to a statement, theory, or finding.

Synonyms: Verify, endorse

1. It has already been corroborated that my proposal has a high possibility of being an effective project to attract new customers.

2. Scientists have discovered evidence that might corroborate the existence of aliens.

Cosmopolitan

Having worldwide scope or influence; familiar with and at ease in many different countries and cultures.

Synonyms: Charitable, compassionate

65

Adj.

1. Her cosmopolitan lifestyle was shaped by years of living in Paris, Tokyo, and New York.

2. The city had a cosmopolitan feel, with international restaurants on every corner and people speaking dozens of languages

Culpable

Deserving blame or responsibility for a wrongdoing.

Synonyms: Guilty, blameable

66

Adj.

1. The investigation revealed that he was culpable for the accident.

2. She felt culpable for not speaking up sooner when she saw the mistake.

Cursory

Hasty and therefore not thorough or detailed.

Synonyms: Casual, superficial

1. His cursory glance at the report missed several important details.

2. She gave a cursory nod to the idea but didn't seem fully convinced.

Daunt

To make someone feel intimidated or discouraged.

Synonyms: Abash, shake

1. Despite the challenges ahead, nothing could daunt her determination to succeed.

2. The difficult task did not daunt him; he tackled it with determination.

Debilitate

To weaken or impair.

Synonyms: Intentional, calculated

69

Verb

1. The long illness began to debilitate him, leaving him too weak to go to work.

2. The harsh winter weather debilitated the crops, leading to a poor harvest.

Decorous

Proper; in good taste.

Synonyms: Seemly, decent

70

Adj.

1. The guest maintained a decorous demeanor throughout the visit.

2. His decorous behavior at the ceremony impressed everyone.

Deference

Humble submission or respect.

Synonyms: Regard, respect

Noun

1. In many Asian cultures, people bow to show their deference to the other person.

2. In deference to the family traditions, he waited for his grandparents to pray before dinner.

Defunct

No longer existing or functioning.

Synonyms: Unused, extinct

Adj.

1. The old factory is now defunct, with its machinery covered in dust.

2. That social media platform is practically defunct, with very few active users remaining.

Deleterious

Harmful or damaging.

Synonyms: Detrimental, hurtful

73

Adj.

⭐

1. Smoking has a deleterious effect on your health, increasing the risk of various diseases.

2. The pollution from the factory had a deleterious impact on the local wildlife.

Delineate

To describe or portray precisely.

Synonyms: Accurate, correct

74

Verb

1. The artist used bold lines to delineate the boundaries of the landscape in the painting.

2. The report clearly delineates the steps required to improve the company's performance over the next year.

Demure

Reserved, modest, or shy.

Synonyms: Introverted, shy

1. Her demure smile hid the confidence she felt inside.

2. Her demure demeanor often hid her quick wit and sharp intelligence.

Denounce

To publicly declare wrong or evil.

Synonyms: Condemn, criticize

1. The politician denounced the corruption in the government during his speech.

2. She publicly denounced the company's unethical practices, calling for a boycott.

Deprecate

To express disapproval of.

Synonyms: Disapprove, belittle

1. The teacher deprecated the student's habit of turning in assignments late

2. We should deprecate the excessive use of plastic to save the environment.

Verb

Deride

To mock or ridicule.

Synonyms: Mock, joke

1. She no longer paints after her school teacher derided her painting in front of the class.

2. Although he led the country to prosperity, he was derided multiple times by the people.

Verb

Despot

A ruler with absolute power, often cruel or oppressive.

Synonyms: Abuse, power

1. The despot ruled with an iron fist, silencing any opposition to his authority.

2. Throughout history, many despots have been overthrown by revolutions.

Depravity

Moral corruption or wickedness.

Synonyms: Corrupt, pollute

1. The depravity of the crime left the community in disbelief.

2. The novel explored human depravity through its dark and twisted characters.

Detrimental

Harmful or damaging.

Synonyms: Harm, negative

Adj.

1. Prolonged exposure to high levels of stress can be detrimental to both your mental and physical health.

2. The company's decision to cut corners on safety measures proved to be detrimental in the long run.

Dichotomy

A division or contrast between two things.

Synonyms: Comparison, contrast

Noun

1. These is a clear dichotomy between his public persona and private life.

2. There is a stark dichotomy between his professional success and personal struggles.

Discrepancy

A lack of agreement or consistency.

Synonyms: Deviation, mismatch

83

Noun

1. There was a discrepancy between the two reports, which led to confusion about the facts.

2. The discrepancy in their stories made the police suspicious of their involvement in the crime.

Disdain

The feeling that someone or something is unworthy of one's consideration or respect.

Synonyms: Scorn, disrespect

84

Noun

1. She looked at the messy room with disdain, unwilling to clean it herself.

2. He disdained the idea of working for a company he considered unethical.

Disparage

To speak of someone or something in a negative way.

Synonyms: Desire, hope

1. She aspires to become a doctor and help underserved communities around the world.

2. Many young athletes aspire to compete in the Olympics one day, dedicating years to training.

Dispel

To drive away or scatter.

Synonyms: Dismiss, Banish

1. The professor worked hard to dispel common misconceptions about climate change.

2. A few kind words were enough to dispel her fears about the upcoming test.

Disseminate

To spread or disperse something, especially information.

Synonyms: Publicize, Circulate

Verb

⭐

1. The organization works to disseminate information about climate change to raise awareness.

2. The news outlet used social media to disseminate the latest updates on the event.

Dissent

To disagree, especially with a widely held opinion.

Synonyms: Conciseness, succinctness

Noun

⭐

1. Although most of the board members agreed with the proposal, one member voiced their dissent, citing concerns over its long-term impact.

2. The peaceful protest was a form of dissent against the new government policy, calling for change.

Divergent

Tending to be different or develop in different directions.

Synonyms: Deviating, unaligned

89

Adj.

1. Their divergent opinions on the issue led to a heated debate.

2. Their divergent views on the project led to a lot of disagreement during the meeting.

Docile

Easily managed or submissive.

Synonyms: Compliant, meek

90

Adj.

1. The docile puppy followed its owner's commands without hesitation.

2. Although the horse was docile, it required a gentle touch from the rider.

Dogmatic

Stubbornly opinionated or assertive in an unwarranted manner.

Synonyms: Rigid, inflexible

91

Adj.

1. His dogmatic views hindered open discussion

2. Her dogmatic parenting style left little room for her children's individuality.

Dubious

Hesitant or doubtful.

Synonyms: Unsure, uncertain

92

Adj.

1. The judge was dubious about accepting the testimony from the witness who seemed confused.

2. Her dubious answer made her seem even more suspicious

Ebullient

Enthusiastic and full of energy.

Synonyms: Elated, joyful

93

Adj.

1. Her ebullient personality made her the center of attention at every party.

2. Despite the challenges, he remained ebullient, always finding reasons to smile.

Eccentric

Unconventional or odd.

Synonyms: Peculiar, unorthodox

94

Adj.

1. His eccentric behavior at the party made everyone laugh, as he wore a suit made of balloons.

2.The artist was known for her eccentric style, always using unusual colors and materials.

Eclectic

Choosing from a variety of sources.

Synonyms: Broad, diverse

Adj.

1. Her music collection is eclectic, ranging from classical symphonies to modern indie rock.

2. The restaurant's menu is eclectic, offering dishes from Italian, Mexican, and Japanese cuisines all under one roof.

Edify

To instruct or improve morally or intellectually.

Synonyms: Guide, inspire

Verb

1. The teacher's goal was to edify her students, helping them grow both academically and personally.

2. Her speech was designed to edify the audience and inspire them to take action.

Efface

To erase or make inconspicuous.

Synonyms: Delete, remove

97

Verb

1. The passing of time had effaced the names on the old tombstones.

2. He tried to efface all traces of his involvement in the project to avoid being blamed.

Effervescent

Full of energy or lively.

Synonyms: Enthusiastic, cheerful

98

Adj.

1. The effervescent soda tickled my tongue with its bubbles

2. Her effervescent personality made her the life of the party.

Egregious

Outstandingly bad or shocking.

Synonyms: Atrocious, heinous

99

Adj.

⭐

1. The team responsible for the egregious failure ended up being disbanded.

2. The entrepreneur gave a speech about how he overcame the egregious poverty of his childhood.

◆

Elicit

To draw out a response or answer.

Synonyms: Extract, evoke

100

Verb

⭐

1. The detective tried to elicit information from the suspect without revealing too much.

2. Her heartfelt speech managed to elicit tears from the audience.

350 SAT® VOCAB

51-100 REVIEW

Multiple Choice Synonyms

1. What is a synonym of *concur*?

a) argue
b) disagree
c) agree
d) oppose

2. What is a synonym of *copious*?

a) sparse
b) plentiful
c) rare
d) tiny

3. What is a synonym of *culpable*?

a) innocent
b) guilty
c) carefree
d) harmless

4. What is a synonym of *deride*?

a) praise
b) encourage
c) mock
d) irritate

Fill-in-the-Blank

5. The CEO tried to _____ responsibility for the failure, but the evidence clearly showed he was to blame.

a) coerce   b) edify   c) efface   d) corroborate

6. The politician's argument was so _____ and well–reasoned that even his opponents had to acknowledge its strength.

a) cogent   b) cursory   c) dubious   d) demure

7. The lobbyist's use of legal _____ delayed the vote for months.

a) eclectic   b) dogmatic   c) demure   d) defunct

True or False

8. Her ebullient personality made everyone around her feel joyful and excited.

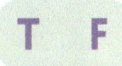

T   F

9. The scientist attempted to delineate the structure of the newly discovered molecule.

T   F

10. The teacher did not condone cheating under any circumstance.

T   F

Matching the words and definitions

Debilitate	Mercy or leniency.
Depravity	To make someone feel intimidated or discouraged.
Daunt	To weaken or impair
Clemency	Moral corruption or wickedness.

Write Synonyms   Write down synonyms for the following words

Colloquial

_____

Denounce

_____

Disdain

_____

Eccentric

_____

Elicit

_____

Crossword Puzzle

DOWN

1. Causing harm or damage.

5. Proper, polite, and socially acceptable in behavior or appearance.

7. Shockingly bad or offensive; wrong.

8. Respectful submission or yielding to the opinion, judgment, wishes of another.

ACROSS

2. To come together and form one whole; to unite or merge.

3. Easily taught, led, or managed; obedient or submissive.

4. Extremely complex and difficult to follow; twisted or intricate.

5. To spread or distribute (especially information or ideas) widely.

6. A strong feeling of disrespect or scorn toward someone or something considered unworthy.

9. To express disapproval of; to criticize or belittle.

Elucidate

To make something clear; to explain.

Synonyms: Simplify, illuminate

1. The professor took extra time to elucidate the complex theory so everyone could understand.

2. Could you elucidate your point further? I'm not quite sure I follow.

Verb

Embellish

To decorate or add details.

Synonyms: Exaggerate, enhance

1. She liked to embellish her travel stories, adding exciting details that made her adventures sound even more incredible.

2. The artist decided to embellish the painting with gold leaf to give it a more luxurious finish.

Verb

Empathy

The ability to understand and share the feelings of another.

Synonyms: Compassion, understanding

Noun

⭐

1. Her ability to show empathy made her a good friend to everyone.

2. Her empathy for others made her the perfect counselor.

Emphatic

Clear in expression.

Synonyms: Firm, vehement

Adj.

1. She gave an emphatic response, making it clear that she would not tolerate any more mistakes.

2. The coach was emphatic in his instructions, ensuring every player knew their role on the field.

Emulate

Match or surpass (a person or achievement).

Synonyms: Imitate, mirror

Verb

1. She aims to emulate her mentor's success in the industry.

2. The young artist seeks to emulate the techniques of others.

Enervate

To weaken or drain energy.

Synonyms: Reduce, debilitate

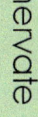

Verb

1. The players were completely enervated after losing three consecutive games.

2. Their project was to enervate the influence of their political opponent.

Engender

To cause or give rise to.

Synonyms: Produce, generate

1. The policy changes engendered both support and criticism from the public.

2. His careless words engendered unnecessary conflict among his friends.

Enigmatic

Mysterious or difficult to understand

Synonyms: Puzzling, inexplicable

1. The old castle had an enigmatic aura, as if it held untold secrets.

2. The detective was drawn to the case because of its enigmatic clues.

Ephemeral

Lasting for a very short time.

Synonyms: Fleeting, transient

1. The beauty of the sunset was ephemeral, fading away as quickly as it had appeared.

2. Trends in fashion can be so ephemeral, often disappearing before you even have a chance to enjoy them.

109

Adj.

Equanimity

Calmness or composure, especially in difficult situations.

Synonyms: Self-control, poise

1. Despite the chaos around her, she handled the situation with remarkable equanimity.

2. Even in the face of adversity, she maintained her equanimity and stayed calm.

110

Noun

Erudite

Having or showing great knowledge or learning.

Synonyms: Scholarly, intellectual

111

Adj.

1. The erudite professor impressed the students with his deep knowledge of ancient history.

2. Her erudite analysis of the novel revealed insights that others had missed.

Esoteric

Intended for or likely to be understood by few people.

Synonyms: Obscure, abstruse

112

Adj.

1. The professor's class was so esoteric that only a few students understood the lecture.

2. He has an esoteric collection of rare stamps that few can appreciate.

Exacerbate

To make a problem or situation worse.

Synonyms: Intensify, aggravate

Verb

1. Despite the economic efforts of the government, they ended up exacerbating inflation.

2. The doctor was concerned that anesthesia might exacerbate the patient's condition.

Exculpate

To clear from blame or guilt.

Synonyms: Absolve, vindicate

Verb

1. The new evidence helped exculpate the wrongly accused man.

2. The lawyer worked tirelessly to exculpate her client from all charges.

Exemplary

Serving as a desirable model; outstanding. Or (of a punishment) serving as a warning

Synonyms: Ideal, cautionary

115

Adj.

⭐

1. She received an award for her exemplary leadership in the project.

2. His exemplary work ethic inspired everyone in the office.

Exonerate

To free someone from blame or guilt.

Synonyms: Clear, absolve

116

Verb

1. The new evidence presented in court helped to exonerate the man who had been wrongly convicted.

2. The investigation was able to exonerate the employee of any wrongdoing, clearing his name completely.

Exorbitant

Unreasonably high (typically referring to cost).

Synonyms: Outrageous, expensive

Adj.

1. The hotel charged an exorbitant fee for a single night's stay.

2. The restaurant charged an exorbitant price for a simple bowl of soup.

Equitable

Fair and impartial.

Synonyms: Neutral, balanced

Adj.

1. The judge made an equitable decision, ensuring that both parties received a fair outcome.

2. The company strives to create an equitable workplace where everyone has equal opportunities for advancement.

Facetious

Treating serious issues with inappropriate humor.

Synonyms: Flippant, jocular

119

Adj.

1. Her facetious comment during the meeting was inappropriate given the serious topic.

2. She made a facetious remark about the weather, lightening the mood.

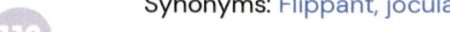

Facilitate

To make an action or process easier.

Synonyms: Assist, enable

120

Verb

1. Installing kiosks facilitated rapid service for customers.

2. Our company is developing a program to facilitate communication between corporations.

Fallacious

Based on a mistaken belief or unsound reasoning.

Synonyms: Incorrect, faulty

Adj.

1. The argument was based on fallacious reasoning and was easily debunked.

2. Many conspiracy theories are rooted in fallacious logic rather than facts.

Fastidious

Very attentive to detail; hard to please.

Synonyms: Meticulous, scrupulous

Adj.

1. Her fastidious nature meant she double-checked every assignment.

2. She had a fastidious eye for fashion, never settling for anything less than perfect.

Fatuous

Silly, foolish, or pointless.

Synonyms: Nonsensical, childish

123

Adj.

1. His fatuous remarks during the meeting made everyone uncomfortable, as they showed a complete lack of understanding.

2. She couldn't help but laugh at his fatuous decision to wear a suit to a beach party.

Feasible

Possible and practical to do easily.

Synonyms: Viable, achievable

124

Adj.

1. Given the resources available, completing the project within a week is not feasible.

2. A weekend trip is feasible if we plan ahead.

Feckless

Lacking initiative or strength of character; irresponsible.

Synonyms: Unreliable, worthless

125

Adj.

1. His feckless attitude toward his studies led to poor grades and missed opportunities.

2. The feckless manager failed to address the team's concerns, resulting in low morale.

Fervent

Passionate or intensely enthusiastic.

Synonyms: Profound, spirited

126

Adj.

1. She is a fervent supporter of Arsenal.

2. His fervent desire to succeed drove him to work tirelessly.

Flabbergasted

Extremely surprised or shocked.

Synonyms: Astounded, stunned

127

Adj.

1. His feckless attitude toward his studies led to poor grades and missed opportunities.

2. The feckless manager failed to address the team's concerns, resulting in low morale.

Flagrant

Conspicuously offensive or scandalous; wrong or immoral.

Synonyms: Blatant, outrageous

128

Adj.

1. The player's flagrant foul resulted in an immediate ejection from the game.

2. His flagrant disregard for the law led to severe consequences.

Flourish

To grow or develop in a healthy or vigorous way.

Synonyms: Thrive, prosper

129

Verb

1. The artist's career began to flourish after she moved to the city.

2. The garden flourished with colorful flowers after weeks of care.

Fluctuate

Frequently changing or varying.

Synonyms: Shift, alter

130

Verb

1. The temperature tends to fluctuate significantly during the fall, making it hard to dress for the weather.

2. Stock prices can fluctuate wildly, making it difficult for investors to predict short-term trends.

Flummoxed

Confused or bewildered.

Synonyms: Baffled, perplexed

131

Adj.

1. She was flummoxed by the complex math problem and couldn't figure out where to start.

2. She was flummoxed by the unexpected plot twist in the movie.

Foment

To instigate or stir up (often related to trouble or rebellion).

Synonyms: Extract, Evoke

132

Verb

1. The leader's speech seemed to foment unrest among the crowd, sparking protests across the city.

2. His actions were designed to foment division within the group, undermining their unity.

Forbearance

Patient self-control; restraint.

Synonyms: Tolerance, endurance

1. The bank granted forbearance to the homeowner, allowing them to temporarily pause mortgage payments.

2. Her forbearance in the face of criticism demonstrated her strong character.

Foreboding

A sense of impending doom.

Synonyms: Apprehension, dread

1. As the storm clouds gathered overhead, a sense of foreboding settled over the quiet village.

2. She couldn't shake the foreboding feeling that something terrible was about to happen.

Formidable

Inspiring fear or respect through being impressively large, powerful, or capable.

Synonyms: Intimidating, daunting

1. The army faced a formidable opponent in the well-trained enemy forces.

2. Her formidable intelligence made her a strong competitor in academic contests.

Fortuitous

Happening by accident or chance rather than by design.

Synonyms: Unanticipated, unexpected

1. The team's fortuitous win in the final minutes left the crowd in shock.

2. Finding the rare book at a thrift store was a fortuitous discovery.

Fractious

Irritable or quarrelsome.

Synonyms: Grumpy, grouchy

Adj.

1. The fractious child refused to follow any instructions, making it difficult for the teacher to maintain order in the classroom.

2. The fractious debate between the two politicians only seemed to escalate, with neither willing to compromise.

Frivolous

Not having any serious purpose or value.

Synonyms: Lighthearted, superficial

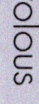

Adj.

1. His frivolous spending on luxury items left him with little savings for the future.

2. His frivolous remarks during the meeting distracted everyone from the important discussion.

Frugal

Economical in use or expenditure; not wasteful.

Synonyms: Prudent, cautious

1. She lived a frugal lifestyle, always looking for ways to save money without sacrificing quality.

2. His frugal habits allowed him to save a significant amount for his future despite a modest income.

Furtive

Attempting to avoid notice or attention, typically because of guilt or a belief that discovery would lead to trouble.

Synonyms: Secret, sly

1. He cast a furtive glance at the clock during the meeting.

2. They exchanged furtive smiles across the crowded room.

Garrulous

Excessively talkative, especially about trivial matters.

Synonyms: Babbling, chatty

141

Adj.

1. You should avoid speaking in a garrulous manner in a business meeting.

2. A group of garrulous old ladies was talking about how to grow pumpkins in the garden.

Gregarious

Fond of company, friendly, extraverted.

Synonyms: Sociable, outgoing

142

Adj.

1. As a gregarious person, he made friends easily wherever he went.

2. Her gregarious nature made her the perfect host for the event.

Guile

Sly or cunning intelligence.

Synonyms: Ingenuity, craft

143

Noun

1. He used his guile to outsmart his opponents and win the game.

2. The thief relied on his guile to trick the store owner into giving him the keys.

Gaudy

Bright or showy to the point of being tasteless.

Synonyms: Garish, harsh

144

Adj.

1. The ballroom was decorated in gaudy colors, with bright neon lights and over-the-top ornaments that seemed out of place.

2. He wore a gaudy gold necklace that clashed with his otherwise simple outfit.

Genial

Friendly and cheerful.

Synonyms: Amiable, affable

145

Adj.

⭐

1. Her genial personality made her popular at every club she attended.

2. His genial smile made everyone feel welcome at the party.

Germane

Relevant to the topic.

Synonyms: Pertinent, applicable

146

Adj.

1. The professor's comments were germane to the discussion, helping to clarify key points.

2. The lawyer's evidence was not germane to the case, so it was dismissed by the judge.

Gluttony

Excessive eating or greed.

Synonyms: Overconsumption, greed

1. His gluttony at the buffet left him feeling uncomfortably full.

2. The holiday season often leads to gluttony, with many indulging on rich foods.

Gratuitous

Unnecessary or unwarranted; given freely.

Synonyms: Unjustified, unwarranted

1. She was criticized for including gratuitous statistics in her speech.

2. Thankfully, we received help from an organization that provided gratuitous service.

Garner

To gather or collect.

Synonyms: Accumulate, gather

1. She worked hard to garner the respect of her colleagues.

2. His speech garnered widespread support for the new initiative.

Goad

To provoke or annoy someone into taking action; or to drive or urge (an animal) on with a goad.

Synonyms: Rouse, incite

1. His teasing words were meant to goad her into responding angrily.

2. She used the stick to goad the horse into moving faster.

350
SAT
VOCAB
101-150
REVIEW

Multiple Choice Synonyms

1. What is a synonym of *fervent*?

a) indifferent
b) passionate
c) doubtful
d) lazy

2. What is a synonym of *equanimity*?

a) panic
b) restlessness
c) composure
d) anger

3. What is a synonym of *goad*?

a) ignore
b) provoke
c) hide
d) accept

4. What is a synonym of *erudite*?

a) ignorant
b) loud
c) scholarly
d) careless

Fill-in-the-Blank

5. His speech was so _____ that it left the entire audience inspired and moved.

a) embellished b) emphatic c) enigmatic d) fallacious

6. The artist's explanation of his abstract painting was so _____ that few people truly understood it.

a) esoteric b) genial c) flagrant d) frugal

7. The league suspended the player for his _____ violation of the safety rules.

a) foment b) formidable c) flagrant d) frivolous

101-150 Review

True or False

8. She was so flabbergasted by the surprise party that she cried.

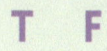

T F

9. His gluttony for learning meant he was never satisfied with just one book.

T F

10. The storm had an ephemeral beauty, lasting only a few moments before vanishing.

T F

Matching the words and definitions

Engender	To clear from blame or guilt.
Exculpate	Silly, foolish, or pointless.
Fatuous	Excessively talkative, especially about trivial matters.
Garrulous	To cause or give rise to

Write Synonyms

Write down synonyms for the following words

Flourish

_____

Flummoxed

_____

Formidable

_____

Germane

_____

Garner

_____

Crossword Puzzle

DOWN

1. to clear someone from blame; prove innocent.

2. secretive or sneaky; avoiding notice.

3. sly deceit; cunning intelligence.

4. sociable and outgoing; enjoys company.

5. to imitate to match or surpass.

8. very attentive to detail; hard to please.

ACROSS

6. to stir up or encourage trouble, rebellion, or unrest.

7. to make a problem, situation, or feeling worse or more severe.

9. irritable and quarrelsome; unruly.

10. patient self-control; restraint or tolerance.

Gaunt

Extremely thin and bony, often from hunger or suffering; (of a building or place) grim or desolate in appearance.

Synonyms: Emaciated, haggard

151

Adj.

1. After the long illness, he appeared gaunt, his face hollow and pale from months of poor nutrition.

2. The old mansion stood gaunt and abandoned, with broken windows and ivy creeping up its crumbling walls.

Grievance

A complaint or resentment.

Synonyms: Abnormality, deviation

152

Noun

1. He filed a grievance with the company after his promotion was unfairly denied.

2. She filed a grievance with Human Resources after being passed over for the promotion.

94

Gullible

Easily deceived or tricked.

Synonyms: Naive, trusting

1. The gullible customer fell for the scam and lost a large sum of money.

2. His gullible nature made him an easy target or pranks and false promises.

153

Adj.

⭐

Genuflect

To kneel in reverence or submission.

Synonyms: Deference, servility

1. Before entering the church, she paused to genuflect in front of the altar.

2. During the ceremony, he genuflected as a sign of reverence.

154

Verb

Gratify

To give pleasure or satisfaction.

Synonyms: Appease, fulfill

155

Verb

1. It is damaging for the brain to always choose activities that instantly gratify you.

2. Parents often bring their young children to museusm and zoos to gratify their children's curiosity.

Grovel

To beg, plead, often in a humiliating way.

Synonyms: Cower, fawn

156

Verb

1. He had to grovel before his boss to keep his job after the major mistake.

2. The politician seemed to grovel for votes rather than standing by his principles.

Gumption

Spirited initiative or resourcefulness.

Synonyms: Shrewdness, courage

Noun

1. It took a lot of gumption for her to start her own business from scratch.

2. He showed real gumption by speaking up in the meeting despite his nerves.

Hapless

Unlucky or unfortunate.

Synonyms: Luckless, ill-fated

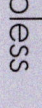

Adj.

1. The hapless tourist accidentally boarded the wrong train and ended up hours away from his destination.

2. Despite his best efforts, the hapless waiter dropped the tray of drinks, causing a commotion in the restaurant.

Haughty

Arrogantly superior and disdainful.

Synonyms: Snobbish, conceited

159

Adj.

1. The haughty look on his face made it clear he thought he was better than everyone else.

2. Her haughty remarks at the dinner table offended many of the guests.

Heinous

Shockingly wicked or cruel.

Synonyms: Horrific, atrocious

160

Adj.

1. The criminal's heinous actions shocked the entire community and led to a nationwide outcry.

2. The heinous crime left a lasting impact on the victims' families, who sought justice.

Iconoclast

Someone who attacks or criticizes traditional beliefs.

Synonyms: Rebel, skeptic

1. The iconoclast openly criticized the long-standing traditions of the organization, much to the dismay of its members.

2. His iconoclastic views on art challenged the conventional styles that had been celebrated for decades.

161

Noun

Ignominious

Deserving or causing public disgrace or shame.

Synonyms: Undignified, obscene

1. I put in a lot of effort preparing for the important confernce, where even a small mistake could be ignominious.

2. The actor faced an ignominious end to his career after being caught for tax evasion.

162

Adj.

Impetuous

Acting quickly and without thought or care.

Synonyms: Sociable, outgoing

Adj.

1. His impetuous decision to quit his job left him struggling financially.

2. She was known for her impetuous nature, often acting before thinking.

Implacable

Unable to be placated or calmed.

Synonyms: Relentless, unstoppable

Adj.

1. The implacable enemy refused to negotiate, making peace impossible.

2. Her implacable anger remained even after the apology was offered.

Implicit

Implied or understood without being directly stated.

Synonyms: Inferred, indirect

1. Her smile carried an implicit message of approval, even though she didn't say a word.

2. The contract contained an implicit understanding that the project would be completed within the year, even though no specific deadline was stated.

Inane

Silly or stupid.

Synonyms: Foolish, fatuous

1. His inane comments during the meeting only made the discussion more frustrating.

2. She rolled her eyes at the inane joke, knowing it wasn't worth responding to.

Indispensable

Absolutely necessary.

Synonyms: Essential, crucial

167

Adj.

⭐

1. Water is indispensable for survival, as no living being can function without it.

2. Her leadership was indispensable to the success of the project, guiding the team through every challenge.

◆

Indignant

Feeling or showing anger or annoyance at something perceived as unfair.

Synonyms: Resentful, aggrieved

168

Adj.

⭐

1. She felt indignant when her friend blamed her for something she didn't do.

2. He gave an indignant look when the teacher accused him of cheating.

Ineffable

Too great or extreme to be expressed in words.

Synonyms: Indescribable, inexpressible

1. No mother in the world could articulate the ineffable feeling of seeing their baby for the first time.

2. The ineffable feelings made me burst into tears instead of describing how I felt.

Inert

Lacking the ability or strength to move; lacking vigor or chemically inactive.

Synonyms: Still, immobile

1. The spacecraft floated through space, appearing completely inert with no sign of activity.

2. The old machine was inert, having stopped working after years of neglect.

Inexorable

Impossible to stop or prevent.

Synonyms: Unavoidable, inevitable

Adj.

1. The inexorable spread of the disease overwhelmed the healthcare system.

2. The inexorable rise of technology is changing the way we live and work.

Infallible

Incapable of making mistakes or being wrong.

Synonyms: Unfailing, faultless

Adj.

1. Although he was an experienced surgeon, he reminded his students that even the most skilled professionals are not infallible.

2. She believed her grandmother's advice was infallible, always leading her in the right direction.

Ingenuous

Innocent and unsuspecting.

Synonyms: Naive, trusting

Adj.

1. Her ingenuous questions revealed just how much she was eager to learn.

2. He gave an ingenuous smile, completely unaware of the trouble he had caused.

Inhibit

To hinder or restrain an action or process.

Synonyms: Impede, hamper

Verb

1. The strict rules in the classroom inhibited students from expressing their creative ideas.

2. Fear of failure can inhibit personal growth, preventing people from trying new things.

Inimical

Hostile or unfriendly.

Synonyms: Angry, resentful

1. The politician's inimical stance toward environmental regulations frustrated many activists.

2. His rude behavior and inimical attitude made it clear he had no interest in making new friends.

175

Adj.

Innate

Inborn; natural.

Synonyms: Inherent, hereditary

1. The scientists are researching whether academic ability is an innate trait of an individual.

2. The innate beauty of nature attracts 40,000 tourists every year.

176

Adj.

Insidious

Proceeding in a gradual, subtle way, but with harmful effects.

Synonyms: Sneaking, stealthy

1. The disease was insidious, showing no symptoms until it was too late.

2. His insidious plan to undermine his rival went unnoticed for months.

Intrepid

Fearless and adventurous.

Synonyms: Unafraid, daring

1. The intrepid explorer ventured into the uncharted jungle without fear.

2. Her intrepid spirit helped her overcome every obstacle in her way.

Irascible

Easily angered.

Synonyms: Irritable, testy

179

Adj.

1. The irascible professor would often lose his temper over the smallest mistakes in his students' work.

2. His irascible mood made it difficult for anyone to approach him, as he would snap at the slightest provocation.

Irrefutable

Impossible to deny or disprove.

Synonyms: Undeniable, indisputable

180

Adj.

⭐

1. The evidence presented in court was irrefutable, leaving no room for doubt.

2. Her irrefutable logic convinced everyone that she was right.

Jaded

Tired, bored, or lacking enthusiasm, typically after having had too much of something.

Synonyms: Fatigued, disillusioned

Adj.

1. After years of chasing success, she became jaded by the corporate world and longed for something more meaningful.

2. He used to be passionate about politics, but now he's too jaded to believe any real change will happen.

Juxtapose

To place things together for contrasting effect.

Synonyms: Compare, contrast

Verb

1. The artist chose to juxtapose bright colors with dark shadows to create a striking contrast in her painting.

2. The documentary juxtaposed the luxurious lives of the wealthy with the struggles of the working class to highlight economic inequality.

Keen

Having a sharp edge or point; also can mean eager or enthusiastic.

Synonyms: Acute, perceptive

1. She is hoping to develop her keen academic interest in psychology by applying to colleges.

2. The blacksmiths work to forge weapons and tools with keen blades.

183

Adj.

Knavery

Dishonest or unscrupulous behavior.

Synonyms: Trickery, deceit

1. The con artist's knavery left many innocent people financially ruined.

2. His reputation was tarnished by rumors of knavery and deception.

184

Noun

Laconic

Using few words; concise.

Synonyms: Short, brief

185

Adj.

⭐

1. His laconic reply to the lengthy email was simply, "Noted."

2. She had a laconic style of communication, preferring short, direct answers over long-winded explanations.

Lament

To mourn or express grief.

Synonyms: Express sorrow, wail

186

Verb

⭐

1. He couldn't help but lament the lost opportunity that could have changed his life.

2. The villagers gathered to lament the destruction of their homes after the storm.

Languid

Weak or faint from illness or fatigue.

Synonyms: Sickly, feeble

Adj.

⭐

1. After the long hike, he felt languid and had to sit down to rest.

2. The languid state of the patient worried the doctor, who ordered more tests.

Latent

Existing but not yet developed or manifest; hidden or concealed.

Synonyms: Inactive, quiescent

Adj.

1. The coach believed the young athlete had latent potential that just needed the right training to emerge.

2. Her latent fear of public speaking surfaced when she had to present in front of the class.

Laud

To praise highly.

Synonyms: Praise, hail

189

Verb

1. The professor lauded the student's research for its depth and originality.

2. At the ceremony, the community gathered to laud the efforts of those who helped rebuild after the storm.

Laudable

Worthy of praise or commendation.

Synonyms: Admirable, creditable

190

Adj.

1. At the end of the year, the school selects five students who have demonstrated laudable behavior.

2. The audience began applauding the laudable efforts made by the athlete.

Lethargic
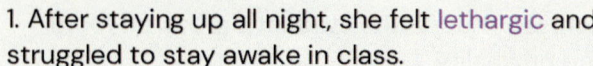

Feeling sluggish, tired, or lacking energy.

Synonyms: Slow, apathetic

191

Adj.

1. After staying up all night, she felt lethargic and struggled to stay awake in class.

2. The hot weather made everyone feel lethargic and unmotivated.

Loquacious

Very talkative.

Synonyms: Chatty, verbose

192

Adj.

1. The loquacious student kept the conversation going long after class ended.

2. Despite being shy at first, he became loquacious once he felt comfortable.

Lucid

Clear and easy to understand.

Synonyms: Intelligible, comprehensible

1. The professor's explanation of the complex theory was so lucid that even students with no background in the subject could understand it.

2. After a good night's sleep, her thoughts were more lucid, and she could finally focus on the task at hand.

193

Adj.

⭐

Lugubrious

Looking or sounding sad and dismal.

Synonyms: Mournful, gloomy

194

1. His lugubrious expression made it clear that something was seriously wrong.

2. The movie had a lugubrious tone, leaving the audience feeling somber long after it ended.

Adj.

Magnanimous

Very generous or forgiving.

Synonyms: Charitable, altruistic

Adj.

1. The magnanimous donor contributed millions to build schools and hospitals in underprivileged areas.

2. Despite the betrayal, she was magnanimous, offering forgiveness instead of holding a grudge.

Malevolent

Having or showing a wish to do evil to others.

Synonyms: Hostile, bitter

Adj.

1. The malevolent glare in his eyes sent chills down her spine.

2. The villain's malevolent plan aimed to bring chaos and destruction to the city.

Malign

To speak harmful, untrue statements about someone.

Synonyms: Slander, vilify

1. It is wrong to malign someone's character without knowing the full story.

2. The sales of vegetable oil decreased sharply after it was maligned in the news for its negative effect on health.

Malleable

Pliable, flexible or easily influenced.

Synonyms: Able to be shaped, ductile

1. Young minds are malleable and can be shaped by their environment.

2. Gold is a highly malleable metal, easily shaped into different forms.

Maverick

Noun

An independent-minded, unconventional person.

Synonyms: Individualist, nonconformist

1. The maverick journalist fearlessly reported on controversial topics.

2. She was a maverick in the art world, refusing to follow trends.

Mendacious

Adj.

Dishonest or false.

Synonyms: Lying, untruthful

1. The politician's mendacious statements during the debate caused public distrust and skepticism.

2. Her mendacious claims about her achievements were quickly debunked by her colleagues.

350
SAT®
VOCAB

151-200
REVIEW

Multiple Choice Synonyms

1. What is a synonym of *haughty*?

a) Humble
b) Arrogant
c) Generous
d) Grateful

2. What is a synonym of ineffable?

a) Unimaginable
b) Expressible
c) Silent
d) Unclean

3. What is a synonym of *mendacious*?

a) Trustworthy
b) Deceitful
c) Friendly
d) Loud

4. What is a synonym of *inert*

a) Active
b) Energetic
c) Still
d) Creative

Fill-in-the-Blank

5. Despite the team's efforts, the leader remained _____, unwilling to compromise or listen.

a) Intrepid   b) Implacable   c) Gregarious d) Hapless

6. After days without food and rest, the soldiers appeared _____ and barely able to move.

a) Gaunt   b) Laudable   c) Gullible   d) Lucid

7. Known for defying convention, the young entrepreneur was a _____ who refused to follow established rules.

a) laconic   b) lugubrious   c) maverick   d) inimical

151-200 Review

True or False

8. The judge showed a magnanimous attitude by mocking the losing team.

T   F

9. Her irascible nature meant she got angry easily over minor things.

T   F

10. He was praised for his iconoclast beliefs, always upholding traditional values.

T   F

Matching the words and definitions

Grovel

Juxtapose

Knavery

Loquacious

To beg, plead, often in a humiliating way.

Very Talkative

To place things side by side for comparison

Dishonest or unscrupulous behavior

Write Synonyms
Write down synonyms for the following words

Laudable

_____

Languid

_____

Inane

_____

Indignant

_____

Keen

_____

Crossword Puzzle

DOWN

6. Clear and easy to understand.

7. Unlucky or unfortunate.

8. Implied though not plainly expressed.

9. Having or showing a wish to do evil.

10. Proceeding gradually and subtly with harmful effects.

ACROSS

1. Fearless and adventurous.

2. Impossible to deny or disprove.

3. Sluggish; lacking energy.

4. Existing but not yet developed; hidden or concealed.

5. Courage and resourcefulness.

Meticulous

Showing great attention to detail; very careful and precise.

Synonyms: Exact, conscientious

1. She was meticulous in organizing her notes, making sure every detail was perfectly in place.

2. His meticulous attention to detail made him an invaluable member of the team.

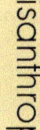

Adj.

Misanthrope

A person who dislikes or distrusts others.

Synonyms: Cynic, pessimist

1. The misanthrope refused to attend social gatherings, preferring solitude over interaction with others.

2. His misanthropic views made it difficult for him to form lasting relationships or trust people.

Noun

Mitigate

To make less severe, serious, or painful.

Synonyms: Reduce, diminish

Verb

⭐

1. The designer used bold colors to accentuate the beauty of the dress.

2. The speaker's powerful tone and expressive gestures accentuated the importance of his message.

Mollify

To calm or soothe.

Synonyms: Pacify, appease

Verb

⭐

1. The brand provided a discount coupon to mollify the customers' wrath after a two-week delay in their products.

2. I attempted to mollify my angry mother by doing the housework for her.

Mundane

Lacking interest or excitement; dull.

Synonyms: Boring, monotonous

Adj.

1. Her stories made even the most mundane experiences sound exciting.

2. The movie was criticized for its mundane plot and predictable ending.

Munificent

Extremely generous.

Synonyms: Lavish, bountiful

Adj.

1. The billionaire was known for his munificent donations to charity.

2. His munificent gift helped build a new library for the university.

Myriad

A countless or extremely great number.

Synonyms: Multitude, a mass

Noun

1. His research opened up a myriad of new possibilities.

2. The sky was filled with a myriad of twinkling stars.

Mystify

To bewilder or confuse.

Synonyms: Puzzle, perplex

Verb

1. The magician's final trick seemed to mystify the audience, leaving them in awe and disbelief.

2. The complex instructions on the project mystified the new employees, who had trouble understanding the steps.

Nascent

Emerging, coming into existence.

Synonyms: Fresh, Developing

Adj.

1. The nascent technology showed great promise, even though it was still in the prototype phase.

2. Her nascent interest in economics grew stronger after she joined the student-run microbank.

Nebulous

Vague, unclear.

Synonyms: Hazy, cloudy

Adj.

1. His explanation for being late was so nebulous that no one could tell if he was telling the truth.

2. The rules of the contest were nebulous, leaving many participants confused about what was expected.

Nefarious

Wicked or villainous.

Synonyms: Sinister, evil

211

Adj.

⭐

1. The convenience store cashier noticed that the customer was about to commit a nefarious crime after hearing him talking on the phone.

2. We are conducting a campaign to raise awareness of nefarious activities occuring online.

Negligible

So small or unimportant that it can be disregarded.

Synonyms: Insignificant, trivial

212

Adj.

⭐

1. The price difference was negligible, so she went with the brand she trusted more.

2. The impact of the policy was negligible, with almost no visible changes.

Neophyte

A person who is new to a subject, skill, or belief.

Synonyms: Beginner, novice

Noun

1. The coach was patient with the neophyte players on the team.

2. As a neophyte teacher, he was still learning how to manage a classroom.

Nominal

Existing in name only, insignificant.

Synonyms: Formal, official

Adj.

1. The nominal fee for the event made it accessible to everyone, despite the high costs of organizing it.

2. Although his role was nominal, his influence in shaping the project was undeniable.

Novel

New or unusual in an interesting way.

Synonyms: Original, unfamiliar

215

Adj.

1. The engineer's novel solution not only saved time but also reduced costs significantly.

2. Her novel approach to storytelling gave the characters unexpected depth and emotion.

Noxious

Harmful, poisonous.

Synonyms: Toxic, perilous

216

Adj.

1. His noxious attitude created tension among the team members.

2. The factory released noxious fumes that polluted the surrounding air.

Nuance

A subtle difference or distinction.

Synonyms: Variation, shades

1. The professor appreciated the nuance in her argument, recognizing the subtle distinctions she made.

2. His performance captured every nuance of the character's emotions, making the scene feel incredibly real.

Obfuscate

To confuse or obscure.

Synonyms: Puzzle, complicate

1. The lawyer was trying to obfuscate the facts to delay the trial.

2. Too much technical jargon can obfuscate the main point of a presentation.

Obsequious

Overly obedient or servile.

Synonyms: Submissive, fawning

1. The obsequious assistant always agreed with his boss, no matter how ridiculous the ideas were.

2. His obsequious behavior made it clear he was only trying to win favor with the manager.

Obsolete

No longer in use, outdated

Synonyms: Old-fashioned, ancient

1. Some historical words have become obsolete and are no longer used in everyday language.

2. Many old scientific theories are considered obsolete due to new discoveries.

Omnipotent

One has unlimited power or authority.

Synonyms: Supreme, almighty

1. The king was often depicted as omnipotent, with the power to control every aspect of his kingdom.

2. While some people view technology as omnipotent, it still has limitations and cannot solve every problem.

Onerous

Overwhelmingly difficult and burdensome.

Synonyms: Troublesome, inconvenient

1. The task of sorting through all the paperwork was onerous, but she tackled it with determination.

2. The onerous responsibilities of the new job left him feeling overwhelmed at times.

Opulent

Wealthy, luxurious.

Synonyms: Lavish, rich

223

Adj.

⭐

1. The opulent mansion, with its marble floors and gold accents, was a testament to the wealth of its owner.

2. She wore an opulent diamond necklace that sparkled under the lights, drawing everyone's attention at the gala.

Ornate

Made in an intricate shape or decorated with complex patterns.

Synonyms: Fancy, elaborate

224

Adj.

⭐

1. The ballroom was decorated with ornate chandeliers and intricate gold detailing.

2. She wore an ornate necklace adorned with sparkling gemstones and delicate engravings.

Ostensible

Appearing to be true, but not necessarily so.

Synonyms: Apparent, seeming

Adj.

1. The ostensible reason for his absence was his illness, but in truth he was just not ready with his presentation.

2. Although the ostensible aim of revising the policy was to protect the environment, it actually aimed to provide fewer items for the customers.

Palpable

Able to be touched or felt.

Synonyms: Tangible, perceptible

Adj.

1. The tension in the room was so thick it was almost palpable.

2. There was a palpable sense of excitement before the concert started.

Panacea

A universal cure for all problems or difficulties.

Synonyms: Cure, remedy

227

Noun

1. Some believe artificial intelligence is a panacea for business inefficiencies.

2. Exercise is often considered a panacea for both physical and mental health.

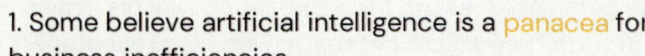

Paradigm

A model or example.

Synonyms: Pattern, prototype

228

Noun

1. The rise of digital technology has shifted the traditional paradigm of how businesses operate.

2. Her groundbreaking research presented a new paradigm in the field of environmental science.

Paragon

A model of excellence or perfection.

Synonyms: Ideal, exemplar

1. She was considered a paragon of kindness, always helping others without hesitation.

2. His work ethic was a paragon of dedication, inspiring everyone around him.

Parody

A humorous imitation or mockery.

Synonyms: Satire, impersonation

1. The comedian performed a hilarious parody of a popular movie scene, making the audience burst into laughter.

2. The show is known for its clever parodies that mock current events and celebrity culture.

Paucity

A scarcity or lack of something.

Synonyms: Deficiency, rarity

231

Noun

1. The project was delayed due to a paucity of available resources.

2. His argument was unconvincing because of the paucity of evidence to support his claims.

Penitent

Feeling or showing remorse for wrongdoing.

Synonyms: Repentant, regretful

232

Adj.

1. Her father was more disappointed because she started to make up excuses instead of being penitent.

2. Inmates have to meditate every day to become penitent for their wrongdoings.

Perfunctory

Done without care or interest.

Synonyms: Superficial, cursory

1. His perfunctory apology showed that he didn't mean it.

2. The waiter's perfunctory smile made it clear he was having a bad day.

Adj.

Pernicious

Having a harmful effect, especially gradually.

Synonyms: Damaging, destructive

1. The pernicious nature of pollution threatens marine life.

2. His pernicious lies slowly destroyed their trust.

Adj.

Perspicacious

Having keen insight or perception.

Synonyms: Discerning, perceptive

235

Adj.

⭐

1. The perspicacious detective quickly noticed the small details that everyone else overlooked.

2. Her perspicacious analysis of the financial report revealed trends that would shape the company's future strategy.

Pervasive

Spreading widely throughout.

Synonyms: Prevalent, widespread

236

Adj.

⭐

1. The pervasive scent of fresh coffee filled the room, making everyone feel at ease.

2. Social media has become so pervasive that it's hard to imagine life without it.

Phlegmatic

Calm and composed, not easily excited.

Synonyms: Poised, tranquil

1. Despite the chaos around him, he remained phlegmatic, handling the situation with ease.

2. Her phlegmatic demeanor made her the perfect mediator during heated debates.

Pithy

Concise and forcefully expressive.

Synonyms: Brief, laconic

1. His pithy remarks during the meeting impressed everyone with their clarity and insight.

2. She gave a pithy speech that conveyed her point in just a few powerful sentences.

Placate

To make someone less angry or hostile.

Synonyms: Calm, pacify

1. I tried to placate my upset mother by writing a sincere handwritten letter.

2. I tried my best to placate myself and remain calm in order to have a logical conversation.

Plaudits

Praise or approval.

Synonyms: Applause, acclaim

1. The actor received plaudits for his outstanding performance.

2. Her groundbreaking research earned plaudits from scientists worldwide.

Plethora

A large or excessive amount of something.

Synonyms: Excess, abundance

1. The library offers a plethora of books on every subject.

2. She received a plethora of gifts on her birthday.

Noun

Ponderous

Slow and clumsy due to big weight.

Synonyms: Heavy, awkward

1. The ponderous lecture left the students feeling exhausted and unable to retain much of the information.

2. His ponderous footsteps echoed through the empty hallway, signaling his approach.

Adj.

Pragmatic

Dealing with things sensibly and realistically rather than theoretically.

Synonyms: Practical, rational

243

Adj.

⭐

1. Her pragmatic approach to problem-solving helped the team stay focused and efficient.

2. Instead of dreaming about perfect solutions, he always took a pragmatic view of the situation.

Precarious

Not secure in place or likely to collapse; uncertain.

Synonyms: Hazardous, perilous

244

Adj.

⭐

1. She climbed the precarious ladder, carefully balancing to avoid falling.

2.Their financial situation was precarious after losing their main source of income.

Precedent

An earlier action or example that serves as a guide for similar subsequent circumstances.

Synonyms: Model, example

245

Noun

1. The court's decision set a legal precedent that would influence future cases.

2. The company's new policy was based on the precedent established by similar organizations in the industry.

Prevalent

Widespread or commonly occurring.

Synonyms: Frequent, popular

246

Adj.

1. Hate crimes tend to be more prevalent when the economy is unstable.

2. Poor hygiene and sanitation are the causes of the prevalent viruses and diseases of the town.

Prodigal

Wastefully extravagant.

Synonyms: Lavish, reckless

247

Adj.

⭐

1. His prodigal spending habits left him in massive debt.

2. The prodigal son returned home after years of reckless living.

Prodigy

An extraordinary person, especially a child.

Synonyms: Genius, whiz

248

Noun

1. The science fair winner was a prodigy in mathematics and physics.

2. His skills on the violin made people call him a prodigy.

Prolific

Producing a large quantity of something.

Synonyms: Abundant, plentiful

249

Adj.

1. The prolific author published over twenty novels in just ten years, earning widespread recognition.

2. The artist was known for his prolific output, creating dozens of paintings each year.

Propensity

Natural tendency or inclination.

Synonyms: Bias, predisposition

250

Noun

1. He had a propensity for staying up late, often working into the early hours of the morning.

2. Her propensity for perfectionism sometimes made it difficult for her to delegate tasks.

350 SAT VOCAB

201-250 REVIEW

Multiple Choice Synonyms

1. What is a synonym of *misanthrope*?

a) Philanthropist
b) Hermit
c) People-hater
d) Optimist

2. What is a synonym of *nebulous*?

a) Clear
b) Vague
c) Bright
d) Logical

3. What is a synonym of *parody*?

a) Tribute
b) Imitation
c) Analysis
d) Original

4. What is a synonym of *prolific?*

a) Unproductive
b) Creative
c) Indifferent
d) Predictable

Fill-in-the-Blank

5. With the rise of smartphones, many once-popular gadgets like MP3 players have become _____.

a) obsolete   b) innovative   c) trendy   d) efficient

6. The chemical plant was shut down after it was found to be releasing _____ fumes into the air.

a) fragrant   b) noxious   c) benign   d) sterile

7. He gave a _____ nod, barely glancing at the instructions.

a) panacea   b) palpable   c) perfunctory   d) perspicacious

201-250 Review

True or False

8. During flu season, it's common for doctors to see an increase in cases of the most prevalent virus strain.

T   F

9. The dancer's movements were light and ponderous, captivating the entire audience.

T   F

10. The manager tried to mollify the angry customer by offering a refund and a sincere apology.

T   F

Matching the words and definitions

Munificent	So small or unimportant as to be not worth considering; insignificant
Negligible	Having a harmful effect, especially in a gradual or subtle way
Obfuscate	Larger or more generous than is usual
Pernicious	Render obscure, unclear

Write Synonyms   Write down synonyms for the following words

Myriad

_____

Nominal

_____

Penitent

_____

Placate

_____

Propensity

_____

Crossword Puzzle

DOWN

ACROSS

1.cure-all remedy for everything

3.calm or soothe someone's feelings

4.puzzle or bewilder

5.widespread commonly occurring

6.new or original

2.spreading widely throughout

3.ordinary or lacking excitement

7.appears across in row

8 out of date or no longer in use

10 as a crossing spine

Propitous

Giving or indicating a good chance of success; favorable.

Synonyms: Auspicious, promising

1. The clear skies were a propitious sign for their outdoor wedding.

2. She waited for a propitious moment to present her business proposal to the investors.

Prosaic

Having the style or diction of prose; lacking poetic beauty.

Synonyms: Dull, dry

1. The novel's plot was interesting, but the writing style felt too prosaic to truly captivate me.

2. His prosaic explanation of the complex issue failed to capture the audience's attention.

Provincial

Related to a province (rural area); having a narrow-minded or limited viewpoint.

Synonyms: Rustic, restricted

253

Adj.

1. He left his provincial village to attend university in a bustling urban center.

2. His provincial mindset made him suspicious of unfamiliar customs and perspectives.

Prudent

Wise or judicious in practical matters.

Synonyms: Sensible, cautious

254

Adj.

⭐

1. Some people think Hamlet is a prudent man, but others think he is indecisive.

2. Considering many possible outcomes will enable you to make prudent decisions.

Pugnacious

Eager to fight or argue.

Synonyms: Combative, aggressive

Adj.

1. The pugnacious boxer was eager to prove himself in the ring.

2. Her pugnacious attitude often led to unnecessary arguments.

Qualm

An uneasy feeling of doubt or worry.

Synonyms: Anxiety, reservation

Noun

1. He felt a qualm of guilt after breaking his promise.

2. She had qualms about moving to a new city alone.

Quandary

A state of uncertainty or dilemma.

Synonyms: Plight, predicament

257

Noun

1. She found herself in a quandary, unsure whether to accept the job offer or pursue her passion for travel.

2. The team was in a quandary, torn between two equally promising strategies for the upcoming project.

Quell

To put an end to, typically with force; to suppress or silence.

Synonyms: Settle, finalize

258

Verb

1. The teacher tried to quell the students' excitement before the big exam.

2 .His calm demeanor helped quell the tension in the room during the heated discussion.

Querulous

Complaining in a childish or whining manner.

Synonyms: Petulant, pettish

259
Adj.

1. The querulous passenger constantly complained about the slightest delays during the flight.

2. His querulous tone made it difficult to have a constructive conversation.

Quiescent

In a state or period of inactivity or dormancy.

Synonyms: Dormant, inert

260
Adj.

1. The forest was unusually quiescent, with not a single bird chirping in the early morning.

2. During the tense meeting, she remained quiescent, choosing not to speak unless absolutely necessary.

Quorum

The minimum number of members needed for a meeting.

Synonyms: Proxy, presence

1. The teacher announced that the school debate club might be disbanded since the number of members is below the quorum.

2. We had to look for another participant since the quorum for the board game was six people.

Ramification

A consequence or result.

Synonyms: Effect, outcome

1. The ramifications of his actions were more severe than he had anticipated.

2. They failed to consider the long-term ramifications of their decision.

Rancor

Bitterness or resentfulness, especially when longstanding.

Synonyms: Hatred, malice

1. She spoke to him without rancor, despite their past conflicts.

2. The debate was filled with rancor, as neither side was willing to compromise.

Recalcitrant

Stubbornly resistant to authority.

Synonyms: Uncooperative, defiant

1. The recalcitrant student refused to follow the teacher's instructions, causing disruptions in class.

2. Despite repeated warnings, his recalcitrant behavior continued to frustrate his parents and teachers alike

Recant

To withdraw a statement or a belief.

Synonyms: Renounce, repudiate

265

Verb

1. After realizing his mistake, he decided to recant his previous statement.

2. The politician was forced to recant his controversial remarks under public pressure.

Reclusive

Avoiding the company of other people; solitary.

Synonyms: Solitary, secluded

266

Adj.

1. The reclusive author rarely attended book events, preferring to stay in his secluded home.

2. She led a reclusive life, spending most of her time reading and painting in solitude.

Rectify

To correct or make right.

Synonyms: Revise, repair

267

Verb

⭐

1. The technician worked quickly to rectify the issue with the server, restoring service within an hour.

2. She apologized and took steps to rectify the mistake by offering a refund to the customer.

Redolent

Strongly reminiscent or suggestive of something.

Synonyms: Fragrant, evocative

268

Adj.

1. The aroma of freshly baked cookies, redolent of my childhood, filled the entire house.

2. This song is redolent of the summer I spent in Hawaii.

Rejuvenate

To make younger or more lively.

Synonyms: Revitalize, refresh

269

Verb

1. The vacation helped rejuvenate her mind and body.

2. The new policies were designed to rejuvenate the economy.

Relegate

To assign to a lower position or place.

Synonyms: Downgrade, demote

270

Verb

1. After the team's poor performance, they were relegated to a lower division.

2. The manager decided to relegate the minor tasks to his assistant.

Reprehensible

Deserving censure or disapproval.

Synonyms: Deplorable, disgraceful

271

Adj.

1. Lying to your friends to avoid trouble is reprehensible and shows a lack of integrity.

2. The teacher said her rude and hurtful comments were completely reprehensible and unacceptable in class.

Reproach

The expression of disapproval or disappointment.

Synonyms: Rebuke, reprimand

272

Noun
Verb

1. She gave him a look of reproach when he arrived late to the meeting.

2 .His actions were met with reproach from his colleagues, who expected better behavior.

Repudiate

Refuse to accept or be associated with.

Synonyms: Reject, renounce

1. He repudiated the stereotypes that people often assumed about his profession.

2. The teacher encouraged students to repudiate unfounded rumors and focus on facts.

273

Verb

Rescind

Revoke, cancel, or repeal (a law, order, or agreement).

Synonyms: Annul, abolish

1. The company decided to rescind the job offer after discovering discrepancies in the applicant's resume.

2. The judge ruled to rescind the previous decision, leading to a retrial of the case.

274

Verb

Resilient

Able to recover quickly from difficulties.

Synonyms: Strong, tough

275

Adj.

⭐

1. Despite the many challenges she faced, her resilient attitude helped her overcome every obstacle.

2. The resilient fabric of the jacket withstood the harsh winter conditions without tearing.

Reticent

Reserved, reluctant to speak.

Synonyms: Quiet, withdrawn

276

Adj.

1. Although she was reticent at first, she now openly shares her personal life.

2. I do not enjoy meeting new people because of my reticent personality.

Sacrosanct

(Of a principle, place, or routine) regarded as too important or valuable to be <u>interfered</u> with.

Synonyms: Sacred, respected

277

Adj.

1. In their culture, family traditions are considered sacrosanct and must be respected.

2. The Constitution is often viewed as a sacrosanct document that should not be altered lightly.

Sagacious

Having or showing keen judgment or discernment.

Synonyms: Shrewd, wise

278

Adj.

1. The sagacious professor always gave insightful advice to his students.

2. Her sagacious decision saved the company from financial ruin.

Salient

Most noticeable or important.

Synonyms: Principal, main

279

Adj.

⭐

1. The most salient feature of the painting was the vibrant use of color, which drew the viewer's attention immediately.

2. During the meeting, she highlighted the salient points of the proposal, ensuring everyone understood its key objectives.

Sanguine

Optimistic or positive, especially in an apparently bad or difficult situation.

Synonyms: Optimistic, hopeful

280

Adj.

⭐

1. Despite the challenges ahead, she remained sanguine about the future of her startup.

2. His sanguine outlook helped the team stay motivated even during tough times.

Sardonic

Grimly mocking.

Synonyms: Scornful, sarcastic

Adj.

1. His sardonic smile hinted that he didn't take the situation seriously, even though everyone else was worried.

2. She made a sardonic comment about the company's new policy, clearly unimpressed with the changes.

Scrupulous

Meticulous or thorough; attentive to detail.

Synonyms: Careful, conscientious

Adj.

1. The accountant was scrupulous to ensure that every transaction was recorded accurately.

2. Having a scrupulous crew help my clothing business prevents faulty items from being shipped to customers.

Scrutinize

Examine or inspect closely and thoroughly.

Synonyms: Scan, investigate

283

Verb

1. . The teacher carefully scrutinized each essay for plagiarism before grading.

2. Scientists must scrutinize every result to ensure the data is accurate and reliable.

Soporific

Causing sleepiness.

Synonyms: Sleep-inducing, drowsy

284

Adj.

1. The professor's monotonous lecture was so soporific that several students fell asleep.

2. A warm cup of chamomile tea can have a soporific effect before bedtime.

Sporadic

Occurring irregularly; scattered or isolated.

Synonyms: Infrequent, periodical

1. His visits to the gym were sporadic, so he saw little progress.

2. The internet connection was sporadic, making it hard to complete work.

Spurious

False, not genuine.

Synonyms: Untrue, fraudulent

1. The spurious claims made by the company were quickly debunked by independent experts.

2. He was cautious about accepting the spurious advice, knowing it could lead to disastrous results.

Squalid

(Of a place) extremely dirty and unpleasant, especially as a result of poverty or neglect.

Synonyms: Dirty, filthy

1. The abandoned house was in a squalid condition, with broken windows and rotting furniture.

2. They couldn't ignore the squalid living conditions in the refugee camp any longer.

Stolid

Unemotional, showing little emotion.

Synonyms: Calm, dull

1. His stolid expression made it hard to tell if he was upset or simply uninterested in the conversation.

2. Despite the chaos around him, he remained stolid, not showing any signs of stress or anxiety.

Stringent

Strict, precise, and exacting.

Synonyms: Harsh, tough

1. The school has stringent rules about academic honesty, and even minor violations can lead to suspension.

2. Due to stringent safety regulations, all equipment must be inspected daily before use.

Subjugate

To dominate; conquer.

Synonyms: Defeat, crush

1. The dictator's goal was to subjugate the neighboring the countries within two years.

2.He refuses to subjugate his opinion just to fit in with the group.

Subterfuge

Deceit used to achieve a goal.

Synonyms: Trickery, craft

Noun

1. He used subterfuge to gain access to the classified documents.

2.Her charm was merely a subterfuge to manipulate people into trusting her.

Succinct

Briefly and clearly expressed.

Synonyms: Short, concise

Adj.

1. Her succinct explanation clarified the entire concept in just a few words.

2. He gave a succinct summary of the meeting, covering all key points in under a minute.

Superficial

Shallow, lacking depth

Synonyms: Surface, slight

1. His apology felt superficial, as if he didn't truly mean it.

2. The damage to the car was only superficial, with a few scratches.

Adj.

Surmise

Suppose that something is true without having evidence to confirm it.

Synonyms: Guess, Infer

294

Verb

1. From the look on her face, I could surmise that something was wrong.

2. The detective had to surmise the motive based on limited evidence.

Surreptitious

Acting in a stealthy or sneaky way.

Synonyms: Sneaky, clandestine

295

Adj.

⭐

1. The students exchanged surreptitious glances during the test, trying to cheat without being caught.

2. His surreptitious actions, sneaking around after hours, raised suspicions among the staff.

Tacit

Understood or implied without being stated

Synonyms: Implicit, Inferred

296

Adj.

⭐

1.There was a tacit understanding between them that they would work together without needing to discuss everything.

2. His tacit approval was all that was needed to move forward with the project.

Taciturn

Reserved or uncommunicative in speech.

Synonyms: Withdrawn, Reticent

1.The taciturn man rarely spoke at meetings, preferring to listen rather than contribute.

2.Her taciturn nature made it difficult for others to get to know her well.

Tangential

Only slightly related; off-topic.

Synonyms: Peripheral, Irrelevant

1. His tangential comments during the meeting diverted the discussion away from the main topic.

2. The professor's tangential reference to a historical event only briefly touched on the subject, but it piqued the students' interest.

Tantamount

Equivalent in seriousness or effect

Synonyms: Synonymous, Identical

299

Adj.

1. Missing the lecture in the morning was tantamount to falling behind in the course.

2. Drinking a can of soft drink is tantamount to having three tablespoons of sugar.

Tenacious

Tending to keep a firm hold on something; persistent.

Synonyms: Forceful, determined

300

Adj.

1. Despite the difficulties, she remained tenacious in pursuing her dreams.

2. The athlete's tenacious spirit helped him win the championship.

350 SAT® VOCAB

251-300 REVIEW

Multiple Choice Synonyms

1. What is a synonym of recalcitrant?

a) Submissive
b) Defiant
c) Timid
d) Passive

2. What is a synonym of sardonic?

a) Cheerful
b) Sincere
c) Mocking
d) Innocent

3. What is a synonym of *succinct*?

a) Wordy
b) Clear
c) Brief
d) Repetitive

4. What is a synonym of *rescind?*

a) Enforce
b) Approve
c) Withdraw
d) Repeat

Fill-in-the-Blank

5. The general's decision to _____ the rebel faction was met with international criticism.

a) rejuvenate   b) subjugate   c) surmise   d) recant

6. Despite her calm appearance, she had no _____ about confronting the director about his unfair policies.

a) qualm   b) penchant   c) quandary   d) tangent

7. Investigators later found the "evidence" was _____ and had been fabricated.

a) panacea   b) palpable   c) perfunctory   d) perspicacious

True or False

8. The scientist had a quandary when he had to choose from two ethical but conflicting research paths.

T F

9. His tenacious personality made him give up quickly when he faced the first obstacle.

T F

10. Her reproach of the student was a kind compliment meant to boost their confidence.

T F

Matching the words and definitions

Provincial	A consequence or result, often one that complicates a situation or decision.
Sacrosanct	Concerned only with the local or narrow views; lacking broad-mindedness.
Ramification	Only slightly connected; diverging from the main point or topic.
Tangential	Regarded as too important or valuable to be interfered with; sacred.

Write Synonyms   Write down synonyms for the following words

Repudiate

_____

Rectify

_____

Recant

_____

Redolent

_____

Pugnacious

_____

Crossword Puzzle

DOWN

7. Habitually silent or sparing of speech; reserved.

8. Persistent and determined; not easily giving up.

9. To put an end to; suppress; calm.

10. Reserved; not inclined to speak freely.

ACROSS

1. A state of uncertainty or dilemma.

2. False or not genuine.

3. Deceit used to achieve a goal.

4. Most noticeable or important.

5. Able to recover quickly from difficulties; adaptable.

Tenet

A principle or belief, especially in religion or philosophy.

Synonyms: Doctrine, precept

Noun

1. Honesty is a fundamental tenet of strong relationships.

2. One key tenet of democracy is the right to free speech.

Tenuous

Very weak or slight.

Synonyms: Flimsy, negligible

Adj.

1. The connection between the two ideas was tenuous at best, lacking solid evidence to support it.

2. She had only a tenuous understanding of the topic, making it difficult for her to contribute meaningfully to the discussion.

Thwart

To prevent (someone) from accomplishing something.

Synonyms: Hamper, hinder

303

Verb

⭐

1. The heavy rain threatened to thwart their plans for an outdoor picnic.

2. His attempt to thwart the team's progress was met with strong resistance from his colleagues.

Torpid

Sluggish or inactive.

Synonyms: Dormant, lethargic

304

Adj.

1. After a long day at work, he felt torpid and lacked the energy to do anything.

2. The torpid economy showed little sign of recovery, leaving many businesses struggling.

Tranquil

free from disturbance; calm.

Synonyms: Quite, restful

Adj.

1. The tranquil lake reflected the clear blue sky, creating a serene and peaceful atmosphere.

2. She enjoyed spending her weekends in the tranquil countryside, away from the noise of the city.

Transcend

To rise above or go beyond

Synonyms: Surpass, exceed

Verb

1. The athlete's determination and urge to break the goal transcended physical limits.

2. The spiritual unification that music brings transcends language barriers between the countries.

Transient

Deserving censure or disapproval.

Synonyms: Temporary, fleeting

307

Adj.

⭐

1. The beauty of a sunset is transient, lasting only a few minutes.

2. His stay in the city was transient, as he was always moving from place to place.

Trepidation

A feeling of fear or agitation that something might happen.

Synonyms: Fear, apprehension

308

Noun

1. The explorers moved forward with trepidation, unsure of what lay ahead.

2. She felt a sense of trepidation before giving her speech.

Trite

Something that is said or used too often, so it sounds boring or unoriginal.

Synonyms: Vapid, banal

309

Adj.

⭐

1. His speech was filled with trite phrases that failed to inspire the audience.

2. The movie's plot was so trite that it felt like a rehash of countless others in the same genre.

Truculent

Eager or quick to argue or fight; aggressively defiant.

Synonyms: Belligerent, hostile

310

Verb

1. The truculent dog barked aggressively at every stranger who passed by.

2. She became truculent when challenged, ready to argue at any moment.

Truncate

To shorten by cutting off.

Synonyms: Cut, shorten

Verb

1. Due to time constraints, the speaker had to truncate her presentation.

2. The editor decided to truncate the article, removing unnecessary details to make it more concise.

Tumultuous

Making a loud, confused noise; uproarious.

Synonyms: Loud, nosiy

Adj.

1. The protest quickly turned tumultuous as the once-peaceful demonstration descended into noisy, disorderly clashes.

2. After the announcement, the meeting became tumultuous, with voices raised in chaotic disagreement.

Ubiquitous

Present everywhere.

Synonyms: Global, popular

Adj.

1. Smartphones have become ubiquitous in modern society, with nearly everyone owning one.

2. The company's logo is so ubiquitous that you can see it on billboards, buses, and even coffee cups.

Unabashed

Unapologetic or bold

Synonyms: Unashamed, confident

Adj.

1. Her unabashed attitude after making a huge mistake on the presentation made her boss even more disappointed.

2. Sometimes, it is better not to be unabashed and admit your mistakes.

Unctuous

Excessively flattering, oily, or insincere.

Synonyms: Greasy, insincere

Adj.

1. His unctuous compliments made it clear that he was trying too hard to impress his boss.

2. The politician's unctuous speech was full of fake sincerity.

Undermine

Erode the base of foundation of; lessen the effectiveness, power, or ability of.

Synonyms: Erode, weaken

Verb

1. The scandal undermined the politician's reputation.

2. The newest scientific discovery undermined the credibility of previous works.

Unfathomable

Impossible to understand or measure.

Synonyms: Incomprehensible, incalculable

1. The vastness of the ocean seemed unfathomable, stretching endlessly beyond the horizon.

2. His sudden disappearance left the authorities with unfathomable questions and no clear answers.

Unilateral

(Of an action or decision) affecting only one person, group, country; refers to the body too.

Synonyms: One-sided, individual

1. The company made a unilateral decision to change the policy without consulting employees.

2. His unilateral actions created tension within the team, as everyone felt left out of the process.

Unprecedented

Never been done or known before.

Synonyms: Unparalleled, unmatched

Adj.

1. The team achieved an unprecedented victory, winning the championship after years of struggle.

2. The country faced unprecedented challenges during the natural disaster, requiring swift and bold responses.

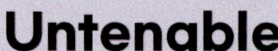

Untenable

Impossible to defend or justify.

Synonyms: Weak, shaky

Adj.

1. His argument became untenable once the facts were presented, and he had no way to defend his position.

2. The company's financial situation became untenable, leading to layoffs and restructuring.

Uproarious

Enthusiastic and full of energy.

Synonyms: Hilarious, boisterous

1. He prefers having a peaceful afternoon rather than attending uproarious parties.

2. Watching an uproarious comedy show is a great way to ease an awkward silence.

Urbane

Courteous and refined in manner; polite.

Synonyms: Sophisticated, elegant

1. The diplomat had an urbane manner that made him popular at international events.

2. His urbane style and polished speech gave him an air of sophistication.

Usurp

To take (a position or importance) illegally or by force.

Synonyms: Seize, take over

323

Verb

⭐

1. The ambitious prince plotted to usurp his brother's position as ruler.

2. Technology should assist workers, not usurp their jobs entirely.

Usury

The practice of lending money at high interest rates.

Synonyms: Exploitation, lending

324

Noun

1. The practice of usury, charging exorbitant interest rates, was outlawed in many countries to protect consumers.

2. The lender's usury left the borrower drowning in debt, unable to pay back the inflated loan.

Vacillate

To waver between different opinions or actions.

Synonyms: Be indecisive, uncertain

325

Verb

1. She began to vacillate between two job offers, unsure of which one to accept.

2. His tendency to vacillate on important decisions often frustrated his friends and colleagues.

Vacuous

Lacking intelligence or thought.

Synonyms: Shallow, vacant

326

Adj.

1. His vacuous comments during the meeting showed he hadn't thought through the issue.

2. The movie received criticism for its vacuous plot, offering little more than flashy special effects.

Vapid

Offering nothing that is stimulating or challenging.

Synonyms: Inspid, dull

327

Adj.

1. The movie was so vapid that I almost fell asleep halfway through.

2. Her speech sounded vapid and had no real meaning.

Vehement

Showing strong, intense feeling

Synonyms: Forceful, passionate

328

Adj.

1. A group of police officers arrived as the protest became more vehement.

2. She is representing our organization as a vehement advocate of animal rights.

Venal

Corrupt; willing to sell one's influence.

Synonyms: Corrupt, bribable

1. The venal politician accepted bribes in exchange for political favors.

2. Corrupt and venal officials weakened the integrity of the government.

329

Adj.

Venerable

Deserving or given respect due to age, wisdom, or character.

Synonyms: Respected, revered

1. The museum displayed venerable artifacts from ancient civilizations.

2. He was a venerable leader, admired by all who knew him.

330

Adj.

Verbose

Using more words than necessary.

Synonyms: Wordy, talkative

1. The professor's verbose lecture made it hard to stay focused on the main points.

2. She tried to shorten her verbose email, aiming to get straight to the point.

Versimilitude

The appearance of being true or real.

Synonyms: Authenticity, realism

1. The artist's painting captured the scene's verisimilitude so well that it looked like a photograph.

2. Despite being a fantasy film, the director worked hard to maintain verisimilitude in the characters' emotions and reactions.

Vex

To annoy or frustrate.

Synonyms: Irritate, agitate

1. The constant noise from the construction site began to vex the residents of the neighborhood.

2. She was vexed by the delays and the lack of communication from the airline.

Viable

Capable of working successfully.

Synonyms: Logical, valid

1. The team proposed a viable solution to the problem that could be implemented within a short timeframe.

2. After assessing the project's risks, they determined that the original plan was no longer a viable option.

Vicarious

Vicarious

Experienced through the feelings or actions of others.

Synonyms: Indirect, secondhand

335

Adj.

⭐

1. Watching the national team win a game gives a vicarious thrill and a sense of excitement.

2. Since the president is unable to attend the conference at the moment, I came as a vicarious representative.

Vicissitude

A change of circumstances or fortune, typically one that is unwelcome.

Synonyms: Fluctuation, shift

336

Noun

1. The vicissitudes of life can be unpredictable, bringing both joy and sorrow.

2. He remained optimistic despite the many vicissitudes he faced in his career.

Vindicate

To clear from blame or suspicion; prove something is justified.

Synonyms: Acquit, justify

1. New evidence helped vindicate the wrongly accused man.

2. The test results vindicated the doctor's diagnosis.

Virtuous

Morally excellent, righteous.

Synonyms: Ethnical, upright

1. She was admired for her virtuous character, always striving to do what was right even in difficult situations.

2. His virtuous actions, such as volunteering at the shelter, earned him the respect of everyone in the community.

Vitrolic

Filled with bitter criticism or malice.

Synonyms: Bitter, causitc

339

Adj.

1. The teacher warned the students that vitriolic language would not be tolerated in class.

2. After the scandal, the public's vitriolic criticism forced the mayor to resign.

Volatile

Liable to change rapidly; unpredictable.

Synonyms: Erratic, unstable

340

Adj.

1. The situation became volatile when tempers flared during the debate.

2. Stock prices can be highly volatile, changing dramatically in a short period of time.

Voracious

Having a large appetite; eager.

Synonyms: Ravenous, greedy

1. The voracious reader eagerly devoured every book on the shelf, always searching for more knowledge.

2. Her voracious curiosity led her to explore new subjects, never hesitating to ask probing questions.

Wan

(Of a person's appearance) pale and sickly.

Synonyms: Pallid, weak

1. After the long illness, her face appeared wan, and she seemed too weak to even speak.

2. The wan light of the early morning made the city streets look quiet and eerie.

Wane

To decrease gradually in size, strength, intensity, or power.

Synonyms: Diminish, decline

343
Verb
⭐

1. His enthusiasm for the hobby did not wane, even after many years.

2. The moon began to wane, casting less light on the city.

Wanton

Deliberate and unprovoked; unrestrained.

Synonyms: Deliberate, reckless

344
Adj.
⭐

1. The soldiers were punished for their wanton destruction of civilian property.

2. His wanton disregard for the rules led to his expulsion.

Warranted

Supported by evidence or reason; shown to be authorized or deserving.

Synonyms: Justified, reasonable

Adj.

1. Her anger was warranted after being unfairly blamed for the mistake.

2. The doctor said that more testing wasn't warranted because the symptoms had improved.

Whimsical

Playful, lighthearted, or fanciful.

Synonyms: Mischievous, quaint

Adj.

1. The whimsical design of the garden, with its colorful sculptures and playful fountains, delighted visitors of all ages.

2. Her whimsical sense of humor often caught people off guard, making even the most serious conversations feel lighthearted.

Winsome

Attractive or appealing in appearance or character

Synonyms: Charming, appealing

347

Adj.

1. Her winsome smile lit up the room, instantly drawing everyone's attention.

2. The winsome puppy's playful antics won over the hearts of all who passed by.

Wistful

having a feeling of vague sadness mixed with longing

Synonyms: Regretful, nostalgic

348

Adj.

1. She gazed out the window with a wistful look, remembering the carefree days of her childhood.

2. His wistful tone as he spoke about his old friends revealed how much he missed them.

Wry

Expressing dry, mocking humor; (of a person's face) twisted expression of disgust.

Synonyms: Ironic, displeased

349

Adj.

⭐

1. Because of his wry sense of humor, no one could tell if he was joking or being serious.

2. From the wry tone of his voice, I could tell he was not giving a genuine compliment.

Zealous

Showing strong enthusiasm or passion.

Synonyms: Fervent, devoted

350

Adj.

⭐

1. The zealous volunteer spent countless hours organizing the event, eager to make it a success.

2. His zealous support for the environmental cause led him to start a local recycling program in his community.

350
SAT
VOCAB
301-350
REVIEW

Multiple Choice Synonyms

1. What is a synonym of *vacillate?*

a) Stabilize
b) Hesitate
c) Commit
d) Strengthen

2. What is a synonym of *tumultuous?*

a) Calm
b) Chaotic
c) Predictable
d) Gentle

3. What is a synonym of *vindicate?*

a) Accuse
b) Condemn
c) Justify
d) Question

4. What is a synonym of *voracious?*

a) Picky
b) Gluttonous
c) Lazy
d) Indifferent

Fill-in-the-Blank

5. After hours of relentless attacks, the hackers managed to _____ the system's defenses.

a) transcend   b) undermine   c) warrant   d) veer

6. His story of surviving in the wild for two months seemed completely _____ to most people.

a) ubiquitous   b) vapid   c) unfathomable   d) vicarious

7. With her _____ manners—light, effortless humor and flawless introductions—the host put even the most nervous guests at ease.

a) unctuous   b) urbane   c) usury   d) untenable

301-350 Review

True or False

8. Her torpid response to the exciting news showed how thrilled she was.

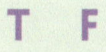

T   F

9. The professor's verbose lecture made it difficult for students to stay focused.

T   F

10. The vicarious experience of watching a cooking show made her feel like she was preparing the dish herself.

T   F

Matching the words and definitions

Wanton	Open to bribery or easily corrupted.
Viable	A change of circumstances or fortune, typically one that is unwelcome or unpleasant.
Venal	Immoral or unrestrained; deliberate and without justification.
Vicissitude	Capable of working successfully or being effective.

Write Synonyms   Write down synonyms for the following words

Vitriolic

_____

Wistful

_____

Unabashed

_____

Transient

_____

Warranted

_____

Crossword Puzzle

DOWN

6. Experienced through the feelings or actions of another.

7. Showing strong and often forceful feeling; passionate.

8. A feeling of fear or anxiety about something that may happen.

9. Polished and sophisticated in manner.

10. Having or showing a lack of thought or intelligence; empty.

ACROSS

1. Playfully quaint or fanciful; capricious.

2. Impossible to understand or measure fully; incomprehensible.

3. Accorded a great deal of respect, especially because of age or wisdom.

4. To shorten by cutting off a part.

5. Having or showing a feeling of vague or regretful longing.

Answer Key

1-50

1. b) relieve
2. c) bold
3. b) dull
4. b) kind
5. a) Amicable: friendly and peaceful.
6. b) Abstruse: difficult to understand.
7. b) Chicanery: "legal chicanery"
   = deceptive trickery.
8. False
9. True
10. True

Abhor — To regard with horror or loathing
Brevity — The quality of being brief or precise
Chicanery — The use of trickery to achieve political, financial, or legal purpose.
Ameliorate — To improve or make something better

- **Abscond (v.)**
  flee; bolt; make off (with); decamp; run off; take flight; skip town; escape;
- **Acrimonious (adj.)**
  bitter; rancorous; caustic; vitriolic; spiteful; hostile;
- **Assiduous (adj.)**
  diligent; industrious; meticulous; painstaking; persevering; tireless;
- **Blatant (adj.)**
  flagrant; brazen; shameless; obvious; overt;
- **Censure (n./v.) (formal, often official)**
  reprimand; condemnation; rebuke; reproach; denounce;

51-100

1. c) agree
2. b) plentiful
3. b) guilty
4. c) mock
5. c) Efface: to erase or wipe out something; to make oneself appear insignificant or inconspicuous.
6. a) Cogent: clear, logical, and convincing; powerfully persuasive.
7. c) Demure — modest and reserved in manner or dress; shy.
8. True
9. False
10. True

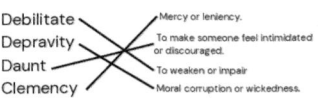

Debilitate — To weaken or impair
Depravity — Moral corruption or wickedness.
Daunt — To make someone feel intimidated or discouraged.
Clemency — Mercy or leniency.

- **Colloquial (adj.)**
  conversational; informal; everyday; vernacular; idiomatic; down-to-earth
- **Denounce (v.)**
  bitter, rancorous, caustic, vitriolic
- **Disdain (n./v.)**
  scorn; contempt; derision (n.); despise (v.); spurn; snub; look down on; disparage
- **Eccentric (adj.)**
  unconventional; quirky; odd; peculiar; offbeat; idiosyncratic; atypical
- **Elicit (v.)**
  evoke; draw out; prompt; bring forth; extract; provoke; educe

Answer Key

101-150

1. b) passionate
2. c) composure
3. b) provoke
4. c) scholarly
5. b) emphatic
6. a) esoteric
7. c) flagrant
8. True
9. False
10. True

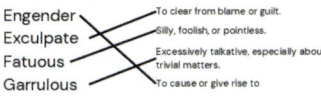

Engender — To cause or give rise to
Exculpate — To clear from blame or guilt.
Fatuous — Silly, foolish, or pointless.
Garrulous — Excessively talkative, especially about trivial matters.

- **Flourish (v.)**
  thrive; prosper; bloom; blossom; boom;
- **Flummoxed (adj.)**
  bewildered; perplexed; baffled; confounded; stumped;
- **Formidable (adj.)**
  intimidating; daunting; powerful; imposing; redoubtable; tough;
- **Germane (adj.)**
  relevant; pertinent; applicable; apposite; apropos;
- **Garner (v.)**
  collect; gather; amass; accumulate; obtain; secure; glean;

151-200

1. b) Arrogant
2. a) Unimaginable
3. b) Deceitful
4. c) Still
5. b) Implacable – unable to be calmed or soothed
6. a) Gaunt – extremely thin and bony, often from hunger or suffering
7. c) maverick — an independent, nonconformist person.
8. False
9. True
10. False

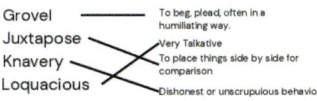

Grovel — To beg, plead, often in a humiliating way.
Juxtapose — Very Talkative
Knavery — To place things side by side for comparison
Loquacious — Dishonest or unscrupulous behavior

- **Laudable (adj.)**
  praiseworthy, admirable, worthy
- **Languid (adj.)**
  slow, sluggish, tired, listless, lethargic
- **Inane (adj.)**
  silly, stupid, pointless, foolish
- **Indignant (adj.)**
  angry, offended, upset, resentful
- **Keen (adj., eager sense)**
  eager, excited
- **Keen (adj., sharp/perceptive sense)**
  sharp, quick; perceptive; eager; enthusiastic; avid;

Answer Key

201-250

1. c) People-hater
2. b) Vague
3. b) Imitation
4. b) Creative
5. a) Obsolete: no longer in use; out of date.
6. b) Noxious: harmful, poisonous, or very unpleasant.
7. c) perfunctory — done with minimal effort or care.
8. True
9. False
10. True

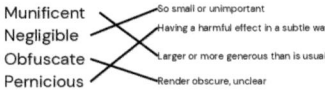

Munificent — Larger or more generous than is usual
Negligible — So small or unimportant
Obfuscate — Render obscure, unclear
Pernicious — Having a harmful effect in a subtle way

- Myriad (adj./n.): countless; innumerable; myriad; multitudinous; abundant; a multitude
- Nominal (adj.): in-name-only; token; symbolic; minimal; trifling; negligible
- Penitent (adj./n.): remorseful; contrite; repentant; apologetic; rueful
- Placate (v.): appease; pacify; mollify; soothe; conciliate
- Propensity (n.): tendency; inclination; proclivity; penchant; leaning; predisposition

251-300

1. b) Defiant
2. c) Mocking
3. c) Brief
4. c) Withdraw
5. b) Subjugate – Subjugate means to bring under domination
6. a) Qualm – Qualm refers to an uneasy feeling of doubt or worry.
7. b) Spurious — false/not genuine; fabricated.
8. True
9. False
10. False

Provincial — narrow or unsophisticated; local-minded.
Sacrosanct — too important/sacred to be touched.
Ramification — consequence or result (often unintended).
Tangential — only slightly related; off-topic.

- Repudiate (v.): reject; deny; disavow; renounce; refute
- Rectify (v.): correct; amend; remedy; fix; set right
- Recant (v.): retract; withdraw; renounce; backtrack; disavow
- Redolent (adj.): (smell) fragrant; aromatic; perfumed · (association) evocative; reminiscent; suggestive
- Pugnacious (adj.): combative; belligerent; truculent; quarrelsome; aggressive; feisty

Answer Key

301-350

1. B. Hesitate
2. B. Chaotic
3. C. Justify
4. B. Gluttonous
5. b) Undermine – To weaken or damage something gradually or insidiously.
6. c) Unfathomable – Impossible to understand or comprehend.
7. b) urbane — polished, sophisticated, socially graceful in manner.
8. False
9. True
10. True

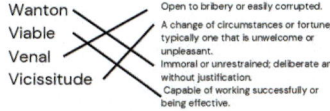

Wanton — Immoral or unrestrained; deliberate and without justification.
Viable — Capable of working successfully or being effective.
Venal — Open to bribery or easily corrupted.
Vicissitude — A change of circumstances or fortune, typically one that is unwelcome or unpleasant.

- Vitriolic (adj.): caustic; scathing; acerbic; biting; venomous; corrosive
- Wistful (adj.): nostalgic; longing; pensive; melancholic; yearning; rueful
- Unabashed (adj.): unashamed; unapologetic; unembarrassed; unselfconscious; bold
- Transient (adj.): temporary; fleeting; short-lived; momentary; ephemeral; transitory
- Warranted (adj.): justified; well-founded; legitimate; reasonable; called-for; authorized

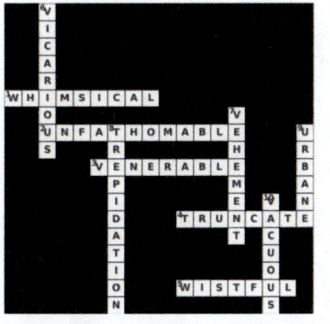

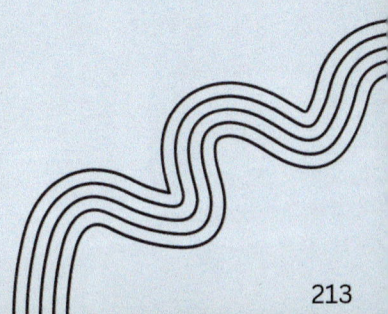

350

SAT

VOCA

-BULARY